ECHOES OF A SEASON

Reflections from the summer

that changed everything.

Wesley Baker

Copyright © Wesley Baker 2025
All rights reserved.

No part of this publication may be reproduced, stored in a retrieval system, or transmitted in any form or by any means — electronic, mechanical, photocopying, recording, or otherwise — without the prior written permission of the publisher and copyright holder.

Wesley Baker has asserted his right under the Copyright, Designs and Patents Act 1988 to be identified as the author of this work.

First published in 2025
wesleybaker.com

This is a work of nonfiction. Some names, places, and identifying details have been changed to protect the privacy of individuals.

Front cover image in window © iStock / Ekaterina Polischuk

Disclaimer

This book is a memoir based on real events, experiences, and people. While it is rooted in truth, names of individuals and some businesses — including accommodations and specific locations — have been changed to protect privacy and respect confidentiality.

Certain characters are composites or fictionalised to better reflect the emotional truth of events and to maintain narrative clarity. Dialogue has been recreated from memory and is intended to capture the spirit of conversations rather than serve as direct transcripts.

The views expressed are those of the author, as remembered and interpreted at the time of writing. Any resemblance to actual persons, living or dead, or actual events beyond those intended is purely coincidental.

*For my family, with my love,
I owe you everything.*

Prologue

My first real taste of travel wasn't exotic or far-flung. It came with the excitement of the open road, packed picnic, and a box of mixed-flavour Crunchies crisps, a travel tradition my dad always made sure to bring along. As a young lad, I travelled with my mum, dad, and brother to St Ives in Cornwall, Brixham in Devon, and Kidwelly in South Wales to name just three. These early adventures, right here in Britain, planted something deep in me, a longing to explore, to roam, to chase the horizon and find freedom in motion.

St Ives was where I first deeply fell in love with the sea, and where I played in the surf. I learned to experience the power of surf there, young and fearless, tumbling beneath whitewater and rising with a grin. The golden arc of Porthmeor Beach, the gulls, the energy of the surf, it was raw, wild, and unforgettable. The narrow-cobbled lanes of the town, full of character and charm, added a magic that stayed with me long after the holidays ended.

Brixham, with its working harbour and colourful houses perched along the hillside, offered something different, grit, charm, and a sense of timelessness. I remember watching the fish being lifted off the boat in the mornings, the seagulls shrieking overhead, the smell of salt and diesel. It was real and alive, and it stirred something in me.

Then there was Kidwelly in South Wales, quieter, more brooding, but no less enchanting. The tide stretched for miles, pulling away as if exhaling, then surging back in with patient rhythm through the estuary. It was a place of long walks, castle ruins, soft grey skies, and quiet reflection. I didn't know it at the time, but these destinations were shaping me, giving me perspective, wonder, and a restless curiosity for the world beyond.

In 1983, that curiosity became a calling. My parents and I flew with Monarch Airlines to Lloret de Mar, on Spain's Costa Brava, my first commercial flight, and my first time truly abroad. I still remember the thrill of boarding that Monarch Airlines 757, the roar of the engines, the excitement of being lifted into the sky. We were travelling with Cosmos Holidays, and stayed in the Hotel Don Juan, the largest hotel in Spain at the time, with over 1,200 beds. It was only a seven-night trip, but it felt like a lifetime packed into a week. The colour, the light, the sound, I felt more awake than I ever had before. It wasn't just a holiday. It was a beginning.

In 1984, we travelled by coach to Blanes, also on the Costa Brava, this time with NAT Holidays. It was a ten-day trip with a day and a half each way on the road, and it felt like a rite of passage. The following year, we visited Pula in Yugoslavia with Yugo Tours, a country that would soon vanish from the maps but never from my memory. That trip stayed with me, something about its intensity, it's sense of change and unfamiliarity, opened my mind wider still.

By then, I was already working. At 11, I had a paper round delivering to 120 houses. I was paid eight pence per paper, not much, but it was mine. Then came Saturdays at Marinair Travel Agency in Whitstable, stamping brochures for five pounds a shift. That's where I met Janet Knox, the kind and patient manager who introduced me to the professional side of travel. She didn't just show me how to work in the industry, she showed me how to love it.

It was at Marinair that I made my decision; travel wasn't just something I loved; it was something I was going to live. One winter, I sat in front of the fireplace at home and wrote to 272 travel companies on green Basildon Bond paper, asking for a chance. A few responded. But one changed my life: Thomson Holidays.

Once I had the name of their personnel manager, I was relentless. I wrote to her every six months without fail.

Then, in 1985, at the age of 15, Thomson invited me to an interview in London. My dad bought me a suit from a catalogue, and we made the long journey from Whitstable. I remember sitting in that interview room, surrounded by people in their twenties, confident, experienced, and eager. I was the youngest there. And it was my very first interview.

A week later, a letter arrived at home. It said, in essence:

"We'd love to offer you a role, as long as you don't grow pink hair or change too much."

In 1986, officially after leaving school I joined Thomson Holidays. I was in.

From that moment, I never looked back.

Over the years, I worked across every corner of the company, from overseas placements and repping to contracting, customer service, operations, product and marketing. I soaked up everything like a sponge. I'd commute from Whitstable, catching the first train out at 5 a.m., switching to the tube, then a bus to head office in London. I'd arrive before 8 a.m., often the only one there apart from senior staff. I had the audacity to knock on the directors' doors and ask, "What do you do here?" And to their credit, they told me.

That curiosity, that drive, it carried me far.

And now, as this story begins, it's 1992. I'm no longer the boy with the paper round or the lad stamping brochures. I'm heading out again, this time with Cosmos Holidays, bound once more for the Costa Brava, the place where it all began. It would be my final visit as a tour representative, though I didn't know that then.

Somewhere, quietly present in the background, was a young woman from southern Bohemia with a beautiful smile, brilliant mind, and dreams of becoming a doctor. Our story crossed borders and lingered between departures and arrivals, part of the emotional undercurrent beneath it all.

What happened next, that belongs to the journey ahead.

Chapter One

The morning began with that quiet, damp chill only coastal England can deliver in spring. A cool breeze drifted in from the sea, bringing with it a fine mist and that faint, salty scent of home. It was Saturday, the 28th of March 1992, and at 8:00 a.m. sharp, I stepped out of our semi-detached house in Whitstable, suitcase in hand, setting off for another summer season abroad, though I didn't know then just how unforgettable it would become.

The sky was a soft blanket of grey, heavy with low clouds and the smell of rain. There was a quietness in the air, not just outside, but within me to. I'd done this before. Said these goodbyes. Made this drive. But this time, it felt different. The kind of different you don't recognise until much later, when you're looking back.

I wasn't packing light either. Not this time. I had my usual large suitcase, filled with clothes, documents, and even my travel typewriter, a companion I couldn't leave behind. It wasn't about essentials anymore. It was about having the tools and comfort I needed to get through what I somehow knew would be a season unlike any other.

My mum and dad were waiting with me that morning, and after loading my case into the car, we set off together for Dover. It was a short drive, under an hour, but it felt significant. Every familiar turn in the road, every sleepy village we passed, felt like a chapter quietly closing. These roads had brought me home after many trips abroad, but this time, they were taking me somewhere deeper than just a destination.

As we approached the port, the White Cliffs came into view, stoic and timeless, standing guard over the edge of England. I always felt something when I saw them, a pull between past and future. Between whom I'd been and who I was becoming.

We arrived early at the Dover docks, just before the 9:00 a.m. meet time. Other reps were already gathering, some fresh-faced, others seasoned, all with that familiar nervous energy. I recognised only a few, faces from a recent training session and February catch-up in London. We exchanged knowing smiles, the kind that said, here we go again.

Our double-decker coach was already waiting, parked neatly near the terminal. Some reps were already on board, having been picked up from across the country on the coach's journey south. Dover was its final stop before the crossing, the moment where all paths converged.

I hugged my mum and dad, one last squeeze before letting go. No big speeches. Just smiles, a few quiet words, and that unspoken understanding you only get after years of watching someone chase the world.

I turned toward the ferry terminal, the wind picking up just slightly, carrying with it that old familiar feeling, the beginning of something new.

At the terminal, I met our coach drivers, cheerful, relaxed, clearly seasoned. We exchanged names and small talk, the kind of friendly introduction that would lay the groundwork for many more encounters throughout the summer. They were regulars on the Costa Brava run, shuttling reps and holidaymakers down through Europe and back again with smooth professionalism and easy banter. Over the coming months, we'd cross paths regularly at drop-off points in Spain, little reunions in the middle of long, hot days.

Boarding the P&O ferry, there was a real buzz among the group. For some of the new reps, this was their first-ever trip across the Channel. You could see it in their eyes, excitement, wonder, and maybe just a little nervousness. For me, it was familiar territory. Growing up on the Kent coast, I'd been on countless Channel crossings, P&O, Sealink, and even the hovercraft. The routine of it was second nature.

Still, I had my tradition. As soon as we pulled away from Dover, I made my way to the back of the ferry. It was something I always did, a quiet ritual, just me and the sea. Standing there, watching the White Cliffs recede, I couldn't help but drift into reflection. I thought of all the sailors who had left this port before me, the explorers, the traders, the soldiers. WWI, WWII, what must they have felt as those cliffs slowly disappeared behind them? My journey was nothing like theirs, and yet the emotion caught me all the same. It always did.

The ferry didn't travel in a straight line, not because it couldn't, but because of the sandbanks of the Goodwin Sands that lay beneath the surface. You could feel the subtle criss-crossing of its path, correcting and weaving across the Channel, part of a route shaped by centuries of navigation. Ninety minutes, give or take. A passage well worn.

I made my way down into the lounge, found a quiet corner, ordered a drink, and just sat in my own company. That early part of the journey always held a certain solitude — a cocktail of excitement and sadness. The thrill of adventure mingling with the ache of leaving behind everything you know and trust. It's a strange pull, that moment. Familiar, yet never easy. You learn not to dwell in it too long. Feel it, acknowledge it, and then let it go.

The sea was relatively calm, no more than a Force 2 or 3, a light swell that might've unsettled some, but to me, it was nothing. A gentle roll. A reminder that you were afloat and in motion, and that life, like the waves, didn't stand still.

Before long, the announcement came that we'd be docking. I returned to the coach and found the drivers once again in high spirits. They'd been down to the driver-only café, a hidden perk of the job, fed and refreshed, ready for the long haul. These journeys ran on rotation, while one driver steered, the other rested, each taking turns through the journey. It was a finely tuned system. A well-oiled machine built for endurance.

Then came the familiar jolt of docking. The ferry doors creaked open, revealing the French coast beyond.

The engine of the coach rumbled to life.
The journey had truly begun.

As we rolled off the ferry and onto the French roads, the energy in the coach was a quiet blend of chatter, rustling snack wrappers, and that low-level buzz that comes with long travel ahead. The highway stretched out before us, and the landscape began to shift, subtly but unmistakably, the colours, the signage, the spirit of the place. We were in France, and the journey had properly begun.

For me, this route wasn't new. In fact, it was exactly the same route I'd taken in 1984 with NAT Holidays, sitting in a similar coach but with very different company. That trip had been with my mum, dad, and grandmother, and I remember her face so vividly, beaming, joyful, thrilled just to be travelling. She sat by the window with a blanket over her knees, smiling at every farmhouse and hill we passed. It's funny how those old trips stay with you.

We bypassed Paris, as coaches often do, skirting the city's chaotic beauty from a distance. I watched familiar landmarks drift by, even catching a glimpse of Parc Astérix, the famous amusement park themed around the comic book characters. I smiled. I remembered seeing that on our family trip and wishing we could stop, but of course, these coaches didn't stop for rollercoasters.

What we did stop for, however, were the mammoth French service stations, often the size of villages. I'd visited these places before to, as a wide-eyed teen with my family, and one memory always returned, the toilets.

It was on that 1984 trip, at a huge service stop in the middle of nowhere. We all filed off the coach and joined the long lines, not just the women this time, but the men to, which was rare to see back home. My father and I went in together, and as I stood there relieving myself, I let out a rather loud bit of wind. My father turned to me, wide-eyed, and spoke loudly, "Pardon me," clearly suggesting I should say it.

But I was a teenager. I looked at him calmly and said, "That's okay, Dad. Don't do it again."

He froze, stunned. And when he turned to the sinks to wash his hands, the other men gave him this look, like he'd committed some awful act of rudeness. The embarrassment on his face was priceless. We got outside, and he called me a "little blighter" as we both burst out laughing. Even now, years later, that memory brings a smile, my father's mix of horror and humour, and the ridiculous joy of shared family mischief.

Back in the present, the coach continued southward, the sunlight stretching longer over the horizon. Fields of sunflowers began appearing on either side of the motorway, vast, golden carpets of them, their heads all turned toward the same fading light. It was a sight I never tired of. You could be half-asleep, deep in thought, and still feel their silent warmth.

As evening approached, I found myself reflecting. Not just on those memories, but on how far I'd come. I had chosen the front seat on the top deck again, the same seats we'd foolishly picked on that NAT Holidays trip all those years ago. Back then, we hadn't realised they were the coldest seats on the coach, exposed and too far from the screen to watch the movies properly.

But this time, I chose them deliberately. I didn't want the distraction of films or the dull murmur of the crowd behind me. I wanted the countryside. The road. The uninterrupted view of France rolling past in twilight.

There was something grounding about it, something that made you feel small and infinite all at once.

While most of the coach slept, heads resting against windows, arms folded across chests, the occasional soft snore drifting up through the stairwell, I slipped downstairs for a break. I'd always liked to stretch my legs during these long hauls, and this time I found myself in the small tea-making area, rustling up a cup for myself and the driver.

The coach was exclusively Cosmos Holidays staff, all heading down for the start of the summer season, and the mood on board had long since dipped into that quiet overnight lull. The driver, wide awake and cheerful, welcomed the tea with a grin as I handed it to him. We stood there, sipping, trading small talk, looking out through the large front windscreen at the empty stretch of road ahead.

We chatted about the journey to come, the hours still to go, the route south through Lyon, and the roads we both knew well by now. It was peaceful. Still. Then, out of nowhere, a blinding blur shot past us in the fast lane, a sports car, easily doing 160 mph or more. It screamed by like something out of a film. Ferrari? Lamborghini? Who knew. Just a flash of colour and sound, gone in an instant.

"Bloody idiot," I muttered.

The driver chuckled and said, "What a silly twollop to be driving at that speed, could cause an accident."

His words were casual, but his instincts were sharp.

Sure enough, minutes later, the quiet night erupted. Flashing blue lights in the distance. Police and ambulance sirens streaked past us, weaving between lanes and disappearing into the darkness. We exchanged a look.

And then, around a bend in the motorway, it came into view.

The wreckage.

Just one vehicle, the same sports car, now unrecognisable. It had clearly lost control at high speed, slammed into the central reservation, and split clean in half. Debris was scattered across the carriageway, the frame crumpled and torn. It was one of those sights that made your stomach twist, that sudden reminder of how thin the line is between movement and disaster.

Thankfully, traffic was light, and we were able to pass through a clear route, guided slowly around the chaos. I looked out the window in silence, the adrenaline mixing with a strange sense of detachment. These roads were usually such peaceful places at night, long, quiet stretches cutting across the country with hardly a sound. Incidents like this were rare… but unforgettable.

I climbed back upstairs, my seat waiting, and leaned against the window again. Lyon wasn't far now. I remembered seeing it's glow as a boy on holiday, peering out from another coach window on another summer evening. Now here it was again, the streetlights painting gold across the motorways, the city sprawling quietly under the night sky.

It was a sign.
A quiet marker.
We were getting closer.

I pulled my jacket tighter, closed my eyes, and let sleep take over. The mountains were waiting.

When I woke, the light outside had changed.

It wasn't harsh, but soft and golden, that unmistakable Mediterranean light that always felt like a gentle welcome. I rubbed my eyes, stretched out in my seat, and looked ahead. The air felt different. The colours richer. The warmth more tangible. We were nearing the border.

As we entered the foothills of the Pyrenees, the road began to climb gently and curl through wider, sweeping turns. The mountains rose ahead of us, jagged and glorious, sunlight washing over their rocky faces and casting long shadows across the valleys below. There was a silence that settled in the coach, not the sleepy stillness of the night before, but a kind of shared awe.

The view was breathtaking.

To one side, endless rolling peaks; to the other, pine-dotted cliffs falling away into deep greens and occasional bursts of wildflowers. The trees began to thin, replaced by rugged outcrops and scrubby bushes more suited to the warmth of southern Europe. The fauna had changed. We were no longer in France, not just geographically, but spiritually. This was Spain's doorstep, and you could feel it.

Outside, the sky was a perfect blue, cloudless and expansive. The sun had real strength now, even though the coach window. The road twisted onward and upward before gradually beginning it's descent. Somewhere high above, the Spanish border had been crossed, unannounced and unseen, but absolutely felt.

And as the mountains enveloped us in golden light, I found myself slipping into a moment of quiet thought.

Who could have imagined that less than eight years earlier, I had travelled this very route as a teenage tourist, arriving through these same mountains with my mum, dad, and grandma, full of wonder. Those jagged peaks had left a mark on me then, and now, seeing them again, I instinctively took a deep breath. A huge smile spread across my face.

That moment, though, didn't go unnoticed.

From a few rows back, one of the new reps, clearly trying to break the silence, called out with a smirk,

"Wesley's reminiscing about a girl again!"

It was a childish comment, and I knew it. But I also knew where it was coming from — nerves. He'd never been to Spain before, and now he was moving here for the summer. His voice was loud, but the fear behind it was barely hidden.

What he didn't know was, yes, I was missing my girlfriend. That part was true. But it wasn't sadness that filled me. It was something else. A calm certainty. A quiet joy that came from arriving in a place that felt strangely like it had been waiting for me.

Our target was Lloret de Mar, and the aim was to arrive before lunch. The timing was important, it meant check-in, it meant instructions, it meant hitting the ground running. But in that moment, none of us were thinking logistics. We were staring out the window, soaking in the beauty of the Spanish coast slowly coming into view.

The first glimpse of the sea appeared just before we dropped into town, a shimmer of blue that stole your breath. I'd seen it before, years ago, as a boy on holiday. But this time it meant something different. This wasn't just a destination. It was a beginning.

The coach started it's slow descent into Lloret, weaving through familiar curves and past roadside cafes with stacked white plastic chairs, there tables waiting for the day's first lunch guests. My heart quickened slightly. Not from nerves, from recognition.

This was where it all started years ago.
And now, it was starting again, only everything had changed.

The Hotel Don Juan hadn't changed. It's towering, confident presence still dominated the street, just as I remembered from my very first holiday there in 1983. We pulled in along the narrow side road, just opposite the older, smaller Hotel Olympic, which looked exactly as I'd last seen it, as if it had stood still in time.

As the doors of the coach hissed open, we stepped out into the warm Catalonian air. It wasn't scorching, just a perfect, welcoming 21°C, with that familiar blend of salt, earth, and subtle warmth that only the Mediterranean can deliver. The scent hit me instantly. Clean, soft, alive. We were all a little worn out from the journey, but you could see the glint in everyone's eyes. Tired, but happy. We'd made it.

Check-in was efficient, if a little chaotic. We were staff, not guests, so the process was brisk. Keys handed out; room numbers shared. This would be our home for the next three weeks, and while the glamour of the hotel had faded over the years, there was something comforting in its familiarity. It was like returning to an old classroom, different, but still yours.

This was the pre-season setup, a crucial period for any rep team. In the Costa Brava, the tourist season doesn't truly begin until mid to late April and runs through until the end of September. In the '70s and '80s, it had been the same, always seasonal, always intense. That hadn't changed. And now it was our job to prepare, update information, check supplier contracts, arrange excursions, prep hotel allocations, and make sure everything was ready for the floodgates to open.

After a quick lunch in the hotel buffet, most of us took some well-earned rest. That night we shared a quiet dinner and kept things low-key, an early night, knowing tomorrow was officially a rest day before the work truly began.

But I had my own plan.

I was up before sunrise, the first light of the day just beginning to glow across the tiled rooftops of Lloret. Quietly, I pulled on my wetsuit, grabbed a towel, and slipped out of the hotel. The streets were almost empty, just the occasional street cleaner or local walking a dog. I made my way down to the beach, jogging slowly, stretching out the stiffness from the long coach journey.

The beach hadn't changed at all. It looked exactly as it always had, wide, open, and quietly beautiful. It's not a soft sandy beach, but one made up of fine, micro-stone grains, created by the natural erosion of the region's distinctive rocky coastline. It has its own texture, its own feel, warmer to the touch, cleaner on your feet, and somehow more connected to the land.

I ran across the beach and charged into the sea.

And then… shock.
The water hit me like ice, 12°C, and I had completely

misjudged it. In Kent, I'd swum all winter in 4°C seas, but the mild morning air here had lulled me into a false sense of warmth. It took my breath away, but in the best way.

I surfaced, laughing out loud, shouting instinctively into the open sky: "Yes! I'm home!"

And it was true. It felt like home.

A short distance down the beach, a local man was casting a fishing line into the sea. He looked over and called out,

"Bon dia!"

It was a Catalan greeting, not Spanish, a reminder that this region wasn't just Spain, but Catalonia, with its own language, culture, and spirit. People here spoke both Catalan and Spanish, often slipping between the two like waves meeting at the shoreline.

I raised my arm, grinning like a child, and shouted back, "Bon dia, senior!"

He smiled, gave me a small wave, and turned back to his line.

And just like that, it began.

Chapter Two

Our office was tucked away in a narrow side street, set inside an old, weathered building that looked like it had seen decades of stories. From the outside, it was easy to miss, faded paint, the hum of scooters passing by, a single metal door that could've belonged to any quiet local business. But once inside, we climbed a flight of old wooden stairs, worn smooth from years of footsteps, and entered a large, open-plan space, full of natural light and the scent of warm paper and old wood.

This was our nerve centre.

The main room was open and practical, with two smaller offices branching off from either side. Desks, filing cabinets, dusty fans, maps of the Costa Brava pinned to cork boards, it was a functional kind of chaos, but it worked. This was where the reps from across the region would gather during the season, once or twice a month, to catch up, compare notes, and talk through the madness.

But for now, it was quiet. Pre-season quiet.

We were the ones laying the foundations.

We started by working out how we'd manage the upcoming arrivals, which reps would be at which hotels, who would handle the arrival runs, and how the transfers would flow. Coaches, timetables, welcome packs, complaint forms, the gritty logistics that made everything else possible. It wasn't glamorous, but it was vital.

Then came the excursion planning, the bread and butter of the role. We needed to finalise which tours we'd be selling, which suppliers we'd be using, and how we'd train the reps to pitch everything from water parks and flamenco nights to day trips to Barcelona and rustic Catalan villages. The margins mattered. So did the timing, the buses, and the contracts. And there was always someone trying to sneak in a better deal for their own kickback, it was just part of the dance.

And this year felt even more special.

It was an Olympic year, and not just any Olympics, Barcelona 1992 was just around the corner, and the whole of Catalonia was buzzing with excitement. For us reps, it wasn't just a backdrop, it meant we'd be seeing guests arriving not only for sun and sangria, but also for the Games themselves. There was energy in the air. A sense of something bigger happening. Like the whole region had been given a spotlight, and everyone was standing a little taller because of it.

It was all happening in that room.

Papers everywhere. Coffee cups. Laughter. Stress. Sunshine streaming through the shutters.

This wasn't the side of travel people imagined when they booked a holiday. But it was the engine that made the magic possible.

One of the first things any rep had to do when arriving in resort was get a real sense of the geography, where the hotels were, which resorts linked together, how the transfers flowed, and crucially, how to sell the excursions. You couldn't promote a flamenco night or a boat trip if you hadn't experienced it yourself. But in pre-season, most excursions hadn't even started yet.

So, we did what reps always did: we shared stories, swapped notes, and passed on everything we knew from past summers. There were maps spread across tables, highlighters scattered like confetti, and a mix of caffeine, cigarettes, and suncream scent that seemed to hang in the air.

We were buzzing to get started but trapped in that strange waiting room phase — busy, but not alive yet.

The office was alive with rep energy, fake tan on fresh white T-shirts, loud voices, side glances, new alliances forming. People jostled for roles without quite saying it, trying to show competence while still fitting in. The more experienced reps traded tips while new ones scribbled furiously, trying to act like they understood what "drop-and-go hotels" meant or how to make a coach express welcome sound exciting after 24 hours on a bus.

We were all performers in training, warming up backstage before the curtain rose.

Once the dust of logistics settled and we'd all been assigned our base areas, I could finally exhale.

I knew where I was going.

Pineda de Mar.

Not the wild, tourist-heavy hotspot like Lloret, but a calmer, local-feeling town. It was Catalan to the core, simple cafés, older residents playing cards outside tabacs, and that distinct pride in identity. It was quieter, yes, but I liked it that way. It had soul.

My patch wasn't small either. I had two core resorts, Pineda and Calella, and sometimes covered Santa Susanna and Malgrat de Mar when needed. That meant juggling guest queries, excursions, complaints, hotel managers, lost luggage, and coach schedules across a pretty wide stretch of coastline.

At the height of the season, I could be responsible for up to 15 properties, though most days I focused on seven solid ones. That was already plenty.

And I wasn't just visiting these hotels, I was living in one of them.

My room looked out across a dry riverbed toward the town, a quiet view that somehow made the space feel more personal. Above me were the maids' quarters, and occasionally I'd hear their laughter or footsteps overhead as the hotel came to life each morning. The room itself was basic but clean, with air conditioning, a decent bathroom, and just enough space to unpack, unwind, and feel settled. It wasn't luxury, but it didn't need to be. It was my home.

Back in Lloret, I also needed to think about how I'd get around. There was no public transport that worked for our kind of timetable, so each rep needed a vehicle. Mine? A red old moped that looked like it had been salvaged from the back of a barn. It still had pedals, like it couldn't decide if it was a bicycle or a motorbike. It rattled, coughed, and grumbled every time I turned the key, but it was mine.

And it worked.

I took it on slow rides through the coastal backroads, figuring out shortcuts, locating every hotel on my patch, and scouting out the best cafés with cheap croissants and strong café con leche. There were moments, even then, where I'd park up, look around, and think,

"This is my life now. This is my real job."

It was surreal. Ordinary and extraordinary at once.

We weren't quite in season, but you could feel it coming.

Chapter Three

A few weeks later, I was no longer settling in, I was fully immersed.

Pineda de Mar was mine. The guests had arrived, the excursions had started, and the gentle hum of pre-season had turned into a full-blown summer symphony. Days blurred together. Heat shimmered off the tarmac. My little red moped was working overtime.

By now I knew every hotel manager, coach driver, waiter, and bar owner within a few blocks of my patch. I could walk into reception with a smile and a nod and get updates without needing to ask. That was the beauty of becoming a regular in a foreign town, you stopped being "the rep" and started becoming Wesley.

But with that came the pressure to. I was juggling seven core hotels, sometimes more, depending on sick cover and staffing chaos. I had to look the part, know the answers, smooth out problems before they reached the surface, and still somehow keep my shirt tucked in.

Welcome meetings. Guest complaints. Lost passports. Broken air conditioning. Missed coaches. Drunk guests. Tears. Tantrums. Toothaches.

And always with a smile.

But this is where the stories start to take shape.
The ones that stayed with me.
The ones that meant something.

Because while the season moved forward in weeks, the moments that mattered came in flashes.

One morning, I was covering for a colleague in Santa Susanna, one of the busier family resorts up the coast. Nothing unusual, a couple of hotel visit's, check-ins, the usual rep rhythm.

That was until Sharon, the Saga Holidays rep, came flying into the hotel in tears.

She spotted me immediately and waved me over with urgency.

"Wesley, my coach taking all my guests has broken down and we can't get another one here until tomorrow, and the hotel is full!" she sobbed.

She was completely distraught. And to be fair, very beautiful. I had a girlfriend at the time, so I behaved, but if I hadn't, I probably would've asked her out by the end of the day. She had the kind of blue eyes that could melt half a bar of chocolate just by looking at it.

I gave her a reassuring hug and said,

"You're lucky — I'm free right now, and I'll help. Don't worry."

We walked together around the back of the hotel to the coach, where a full load of elderly Saga guests sat waiting patiently, confused, anxious, and stranded. It wasn't just inconvenient. It was a disaster. Sharon explained that because Saga only used one coach for the full journey, there was no backup option, no feeder bus. And since the hotel was full, there was nowhere to re-house the guests overnight.

I spoke to the driver, who told me,

"If we can get a good push and pump the clutch, we might be able to jump it."

The problem?

The guests were mostly over 60, kind, but not exactly built for a coach-pushing operation.

So, I had an idea.

I went straight to the hotel pool, grabbed the entertainment microphone, and made an announcement like I was hosting a game show.

"Can all able-bodied Cosmos guests please raise their hands, I need volunteers. If we can push a broken-down coach, I'll make sure every family who helps gets a complimentary jug of sangria on Cosmos and Saga!"

I had arms flying up from all around the poolside, and not just Cosmos guests either. People from other tour operators wanted in to. Everyone loves free booze, especially when it comes in a jug.

Within minutes, we had a small army of volunteers lined up behind the coach.

"Alright everyone, on three... one, two, three... PUSH!"

The coach lurched forward, coughed, and then roared to life.

A cheer broke out.

Sharon beamed and threw her arms around me, giving me a big hug and a kiss on the cheek, to the applause of her relieved guests.

She climbed aboard, waving as the coach pulled away like a slow-moving miracle.

The thing about Saga was they weren't there permanently like us, they came in waves, every other week. So, when something went wrong, it wasn't just a blip, it was a crisis. They didn't have the two-hour feeder coach system that Cosmos did. there setup was tight, elegant, but fragile.

That day, though, we pulled it off.

Together.

With a moped, a microphone, and a few dozen sunburnt heroes looking for a drink.

One story that always stays with me, and still brings a lump to my throat, is that of Mr. Honey.

He was one of those guests you immediately noticed. Not because he made a fuss or demanded attention, quite the opposite. He was quiet, polite, and dignified. But he stood out because he came from another era, a time of impeccable manners, handwritten notes, and pressed shirts for dinner.

Over the span of just seven weeks, Mr. Honey visited the Altura Park Hotel four separate times.

Each time, he arrived the same way, immaculately dressed, carrying a small suitcase and always with a book tucked under his arm. When he left, he'd always drop six or seven books at reception, leaving them for others to enjoy. I noticed it the first time, and by the second, I was genuinely happy to see his name again. I'd scan the rooming list we received from the hotel, always checking if Mr. Honey was on it. And if he was, I did everything I could to make sure he got the same room. It was a small gesture, but he noticed. And he smiled every time.

He told me he'd lost his wife the year before, and the house back home in the UK felt empty.

So, instead of sitting in silence, he chose something brave and beautiful, he booked a seat on the Coach Express to Spain.

"It's cheaper than staying home," he told me with a grin, "and at least I get some sunshine, some entertainment… and a bit of human company."

He travelled during the shoulder seasons, May and June, avoiding the heat and the crowds.

Each time, he brought with him a few Black Horse Western books, those little hardbacks with cowboy tales and lone riders. One day I casually mentioned I'd like to read one. He nodded but didn't say much.

When he checked out at the end of that trip, he left me a bag of them.

I got hooked for years on those stories. Dusty towns, fast guns, quiet honour. They felt, somehow, like him.

He told me he'd be back again after summer. He'd already reserved three more trips for later that year.

But he never returned.

A few weeks later, I received a message via the Cosmos office in the UK, it had come from one of his family members.

It was a letter he'd left behind for me.

He'd passed away in hospital but had asked that a note be delivered if anything happened.

"Wesley, dear fellow, you are, I'm afraid, going to be riding alone now. I won't be back again. Thank you for your kindness, laughter and chats. It was incredibly kind of you to take time out of your busy days to be with me and I am pleased I met you. Thank you."

I won't lie; I cried inside after that.

And even now, more than three decades later, as I write this... I'm tearful and can see his face very clearly.

Some guests were a blur.
Some were a challenge.
But some left a mark on your soul.

Mr. Honey was one of them.

Chapter Four

Surfing has always been part of my soul. From school days onward, it shaped how I saw the world, the freedom, the rhythm, the deep connection to nature and people. Back in the early days, I'd save up for those black-and-white surfing magazines, pages full of glassy waves, sun-faded boards, and golden Californian coastlines that felt a million miles away from Whitstable. But for me, even then, surfing wasn't just a sport. It was a culture. A brotherhood. A way of life.

When I took the role in Costa Brava, I didn't bring my board. I'd done my research, such as it was in the early '90s, and while I'd seen whispers of waves, there was no real information about the surf in that part of Spain. So, I came boardless, curious, cautious, hopeful.

In those early weeks in Pineda de Mar, I developed a quiet ritual. Most mornings, before the heat of the day, I'd wander down to the beach. The tourists were still in bed or lingering over breakfast. The sands were quiet, mostly young Catalan families paddling and chatting while the sea lapped softly at their ankles.

I'd sit there, magazine in hand, flicking through stories of reef breaks in Hawaii, longboards in Malibu, and photos of surfers smiling with wild hair and sunburnt skin. I missed it, deeply.
I missed the culture.
The rhythm.
My beach friends back home.

But the thing about surfers is this: we find each other.

One afternoon, I was wandering a backstreet near the edge of town when I spotted something unexpected, a tiny surf shop, built into what looked like an old, converted garage. It was mostly windsurfing gear, wetsuit's, boards, and sun-faded posters of waves. I stepped inside, not expecting much.

And that's where I met Sergi.

He was around my age, friendly, welcoming, with a knowing smile. He spoke a bit of English, I spoke just enough Spanish, and in minutes we were swapping surf talk like old mates. He didn't just sell gear, he lived surf.

Before I left, he said,
"Come down to the beach later. I want to introduce you to some friends."

That afternoon changed my whole summer.

I met Mateo and Bruno, local surfers, Catalan through and through, who welcomed me instantly like I'd always been part of their crew. They showed me the coastline, told me where the breaks were, when the swells came in, and shared their stories of chasing waves from north Spain to Portugal.

That night, I called my dad.

We arranged through head office to have my surfboard delivered from the UK, via one of the express coaches heading south. It was dropped at Dover, loaded into the luggage hold, and delivered right to my hotel. I can still remember the moment it arrived, and how I walked it down to the beach like it was Christmas morning.

Sergi and the others lit up when they saw it.
That was it, from that moment on, we were brothers.

Sunrises, Siestas, and Surf Gossip

In those early days, I found a ritual that felt completely mine.

I'd head down to the beach at 7:00 AM, before the heat, before the noise, while most tourists were still snoring in their hotel rooms or fumbling with buffet tongs. The Mediterranean Sea lay flat and quiet, gently glimmering under the rising sun. The only others around were Catalan families, mothers chatting softly, kids playing in the shallows, and old men pacing with their arms behind their backs.

It was peaceful, a different world from the resort chaos that would arrive by mid-morning.

I'd lie back in the warm sand; surfing magazine tucked under my arm and just breathe. These were the moments I missed from home, those still, early sessions when everything felt possible, and the ocean spoke your language. I'd watch, listen, and let it all soak in.

A little later I'd pass the first aid station, a whitewashed hut with a lifeguard lookout tower that looked like something out of 1960s California or Queensland, like a shark spotting post from another era. That's where Bruno worked, and soon, the tower became our unofficial clubhouse.

I'd stroll up with a grin, wave to Bruno and the other lifeguards, and just sit like surfers do, quietly, casually, surveying the scene like we were waiting for a secret signal from the sea.

By then, the beach was beginning to stir. Germans and British would start appearing, towels in hand, sunhats on heads. The Germans always seemed to turn a beautiful bronze, while the British... well, we mostly turned into lobsters.

It was the early '90s, and back then the fashion was to use the lowest sun factor possible, the belief being that sunburn was just part of the process, a temporary price for a tan. SPF 2 of 4 was seen as "sensible." Skin cancer wasn't even part of the conversation.

Looking back, I can't believe how naive we all were. We weren't tanning. We were cooking.

By 9:30 AM, I'd be back at the hotel. Sometimes I'd already eaten, other times I'd swing by the restaurant for a coffee and orange juice, a bit of continental breakfast with a touch of English. I loved Spanish bacon and eggs, and their coffee.

Incredible. The secret? Goat's milk. Creamy, rich, full of flavour, like nothing we had back in the UK.

By early afternoon, with my rep duties wrapped up, I'd return to the beach. This was siesta time, when the Spanish paused life to rest, nap, and reset. The heat was heavy, the streets slowed, and everything took on a gentle, dreamlike rhythm.

My surfer crew all had jobs, but there hours flexed. Sergi, who owned the surf shop, would often lock up for a while and join us. After all, his best customers were already on the beach.

We'd meet at a little beach café, sip cold drinks, and watch the tourists bake under the midday sun. Then we'd wander over to the lifeguard tower, swap surf gossip, and stare hopefully at the sea, wondering if the swell would shift, if a breeze would build, if the waves might finally arrive.

And even if they didn't — it didn't matter.
Because I'd found my people.
And this was the summer of everything.

The First Swell

It wasn't long before the first real swell arrived on the Costa Brava. Surf here depended on the perfect alignment of wind, direction, and storms somewhere out in the Mediterranean. When it came, it didn't last long, but it was magic while it did.

Luckily, it was my day off.

I was up by 6:00 AM, buzzing with anticipation. Surfers thrive on early starts, when the wind is light, the world is quiet, and the sea hasn't yet decided how moody it wants to be. I pulled on my shortie wetsuit, grabbed my board – a sleek 6'1" Nigel Semmens model from Cornwall – and climbed onto my red moped.

In Pineda de Mar, it was possible to drive along the top edge of the beach, and I took full advantage of that to avoid the main roads. My board lay across my legs, and at 20mph, I must've looked like a low-flying aircraft, arms outstretched to balance it. It was probably wildly unsafe, but I didn't give it a second thought.

My sunglasses were another story. Made by Style Eyes of California, with leather side covers to block out glare, they gave me a kind of Biggles-meets-California look that I absolutely loved. I'd bought them back in Whitstable at the local surf shop, and every time I wore them, I felt somehow connected to the global surf tribe.

I rolled into Sergi's surf shop, where the lads greeted me with laughter and banter about my wild transport. Soon, we were loading up Bruno's Seat Panda – a tiny, battered car that had been spray painted a questionable shade of pink. It quickly became our vehicle of choice for surf adventures that summer.

Boards on the roof, bodies crammed inside – me, Sergi, Bruno, and Mateo – off we went. As we cruised through town, Bruno waved and shouted, "Bon Dia!" to just about everyone he knew. Locals stared. Tourists blinked. To them, we were a curiosity. But to me, we were living the dream.

We pulled into a dusty parking area in Santa Susanna. The sea was alive. Clean, powerful waves rolled in at 8 to 10 feet, bigger than I'd expected. The lads were amped, scrambling to suit up. I stood back, old-school, scanning the break, watching the wind, the water, the shape of the sets.

It was blowing side shore now, giving the waves an unpredictable face. They were breaking further out, which meant depth – more than you'd expect. This wasn't a beginner spot. I was cautious, curious. And then it happened.

As I adjusted my gear, a gust of wind caught my board and spun it sideways. The fin sliced into the deck of Sergi's brand-new board. A thin, clear crack appeared in the fibreglass. My heart dropped.

I acted fast. Grabbing a lump of surf wax, I filled the crack, smoothed it out, and covered the area with extra wax, hoping Sergi wouldn't notice. He didn't. Not then. I kept the secret to myself.

Out in the lineup, the swell hit hard. Powerful, chunky waves with punch. My little board felt small, under-gunned for the conditions, but I had no choice but to commit. We all caught waves. We whooped and laughed and surfed as a crew. The lineup filled with local surfers, a few girls, familiar faces. It was turning into a perfect session, a dream start to my new life and new friends, was I even here or in a dream was crossing my mind.

Then a huge set rolled through. Everyone wiped out. Boards collided. Chaos.

Back on the beach, Sergi discovered the crack. "Must've been that big one," he said. I nodded, relieved. He asked if I could repair it properly in the shop later. Of course, I said yes.

That was the moment. I was in. Properly, fully, part of the local surf crew.

We took a break with fresh watermelon and juice, sprawled out in the sun. Bruno suggested another spot: a point break. I was intrigued. I hadn't expected to hear those words in this part of Spain.

We loaded back into the Panda and drove along the coast to Malgrat de Mar, heading toward the Delta de la Tordera. The drive was full of sandbanks and dusty tracks. When we arrived, the beach was eerie. Dead fish littered the shoreline, and the stench hinted at a recent chemical spill or sewage dump. It reeked.

Still, we walked on, curious. The waves weren't great, but you could see the potential.

We didn't surf it that day. We laughed, gagged, and piled back into the car.

What I didn't know then was that this strange little stretch of coast would become one of our regular secret spots. But that story, like many that summer, was only just beginning...

Casanova on the Sand

It was a hot and hazy day in May, the kind where the air feels thick with heat and even the sea seems to shimmer with stillness. I had the afternoon off and, as usual, wandered toward the beach with my trusty surf magazine tucked under my arm. It was a simple ritual, sunshine, salt air, a few familiar faces. What I didn't know then was that this day would become part of local legend.

The crew was posted up at the lifeguard tower. Bruno and Sergi were lounging in the shade, laughing and sipping a beer, while Mateo stood up in the tower, scanning the coastline through his binoculars like some kind of surf-spotting sniper. But he wasn't calling out waves. He was fixated on something else.

"Chicas!" he yelled, grinning from ear to ear, and pointed further down the beach.

There, just out of earshot, sat four incredibly beautiful women. Two blondes, a brunette, and one with jet-black cropped hair — all tanned, toned, and totally at ease in the sun. The beach was nearly empty that day, which made them stand out even more. I followed the lads' line of sight and raised an eyebrow.

"What's the joke?" I asked, switching between English and my clumsy Spanish.

Sergi chuckled, "We've all tried. Every one of us. Nothing. No smiles. No luck. They shut us down."

It turned out this kind of seasonal flirting was a bit of a sport, a yearly competition among the local men. New female tourists arrived each week, and with them, new chances to make an impression. But these four had apparently proven immune to all charm attempts so far.

"Go on then," Bruno dared, nudging me with his foot. "Let's see the English magic."

I wasn't known as a ladies' man, but I was feeling confident, maybe it was the sun, maybe it was the challenge, or maybe just the ridiculousness of the whole situation. I pushed my sunglasses up, straightened my shoulders, and strolled over like I knew what I was doing.

As I approached, I could feel their curious eyes tracking me. I knelt down on the sand and introduced myself. their names were Andrea, Hana, Marie, and Anna — all in their early twenties, from the Czech Republic, and on their first ever trip to the Mediterranean.

That got my attention. I had a Czech girlfriend back home and had spent time in the country, so I dropped a few words in Czech just to test the waters. It worked like a charm. their eyes lit up, and soon we were laughing. I switched into rep mode, giving them an impromptu welcome meeting — local tips, excursion ideas, a bit of history about the region. They hung on every word.

Then Hana leaned in and asked, "Wesley, where is the nude beach?"

Caught slightly off-guard, I explained there was a naturist beach down in Calella, about a half mile walk from the train stop.

She looked around, shrugged, and said, "to far."

Then — to my absolute shock — she stood up and removed every piece of clothing. The other three followed her lead. Just like that, they were all nude, standing before me as casually as if we were chatting about the weather.

I sat, frozen, behind my sunglasses.

"Technically," I said, struggling for composure, "this isn't allowed on the main beach."

They laughed, waved off my concern, and ran giggling into the sea.

Anna lingered for a few more words, then followed the others in. I could barely process what had just happened. Four beautiful women. Completely naked. No warning.

From the corner of my eye, I saw the lifeguard tower erupting in movement. Arms were waving. Bruno was doubled over laughing. Mateo looked like he might fall out of the tower.

When the girls returned, we chatted more like nothing had happened. I invited them to my hotel bar that evening for champagne and more stories. They accepted without hesitation.

Walking back to the tower, I did my best to hide the more physical effects of the afternoon's surprise. As I approached, a stunned silence fell over the group.

"You were gone ten minutes," Sergi said. "Ten minutes."

"And they were naked," Bruno added, shaking his head. "Fully naked. We ask you to say hello, and they put on a private show."

One of the female lifeguards smirked and said, "He's Casanova. That's it. That's who he is."

The nickname stuck.

From that day on, whether I liked it or not, I was Casanova on the sand.

Chapter Five

Pineda de Mar was beginning to feel like home. With each passing week, the rhythm of my days became more familiar, early mornings at the beach, mid-mornings spent visiting hotels talking to guests, afternoons balancing paperwork and laughter, and evenings often slipping into something altogether more unpredictable.

The resort itself was far more laid-back than its neighbouring towns. Where Lloret and Calella throbbed with techno beats and neon lights, Pineda hummed with a softer tone — local families dining outdoors, tapas bars filling steadily through the night, the smell of grilled seafood drifting down quiet streets, and the gentle clink of wine glasses under string-lit terraces. But it didn't mean things were slow. Quite the opposite. Life here had a tempo that invited you in, then swept you along for the ride.

During the day, my time was split between hotel visit's, sorting excursions, and dealing with the inevitable challenges that came with managing multiple properties. One hotel might have lost air conditioning, another needed a transfer coach rebooking, and always there were welcome meetings, complaints, questions, and plenty of small fires to put out. Yet even in the chaos, I began to enjoy the sense of control, of knowing my territory, of becoming a familiar face.

But the nights... the nights had their own magic.

Sometimes I'd stay in and have a quiet meal, a chat with a hotel manager or some of the guests or even other overseas reps from other companies or unwind with a book. But more often, I'd meet up with colleagues or friends from the beach crew — Bruno, Sergi, and Mateo — and we'd slip into the local nightlife. This wasn't the binge-heavy bar crawl of the big resorts or at home in Kent, England. It was subtler, more nuanced. We knew the quiet bodega bars where the wine was poured generously, the hidden tapas joints only locals frequented, and the beach cafes that turned into late-night havens with live Spanish guitar and murmurs of conversation well past midnight.

And then there were the stories, the ones that came not from the sea or the surf, but from the job itself. The guest who locked themselves out in nothing but a towel, the family who mistook the hotel for a completely different one thirty minutes away, the couple celebrating their anniversary with family only to realise they'd booked into separate hotels. I began to collect these moments, not just as anecdotes, but as snapshots of a strange, beautiful world where everything was heightened, emotional, and often hilarious.

It was here, in Pineda de Mar, that I started to realise something important. This job, this chaotic, often underappreciated, sometimes ridiculous role, gave me something rare. It gave me stories. And those stories, I was beginning to understand, were becoming part of me, I was evolving, but not like other reps doing the same job, I saw this job as only part of my destiny and not the end role or the chance to party for free as so many others did.

I have always been an outgoing person, sometimes shy as well, but generally someone who would walk up and introduce myself. I often found myself drawn to older people, they were interesting, often wiser, and always willing to share stories that made you reflect on life. Living overseas introduced you to an ever-changing parade of faces: guests arriving and departing, locals going about their routines. It was about learning the balance. Making connections. Holding space.

Reps were known for partying, many thrived on it, but that was never really my scene. Sure, I'd go out now and then, but I preferred meaningful connections, quiet conversations, and time with locals or those few people you truly clicked with.

One of those people was Elisabeth.

She was tall, strikingly beautiful, and a German rep working for another travel company. She was based mostly in Santa Susanna but often worked in my hotel, the Altura Park in Pineda. I saw her nearly every day, always alone in the reception area, sipping something quietly or jotting down notes, while other reps sat further back behind desks, aloof, perhaps a little judgmental.

One early evening, I decided that enough was enough.

"Hi, I'm Wesley, the Cosmos rep," I said as I walked over. "Thought I'd say hello and see how things are going."

The change in her face was immediate. Her eyes lit up. She clearly hadn't spoken to anyone for a while, and like so many of us, craved a bit of warmth and connection. We hit it off right away, sharing a few laughs, much to the annoyance of the other reps who stayed firmly behind their desk, glaring, suspicious, or just unsure what to make of us a Brit and a German happily laughing away.

I suggested dinner.

"My meals are covered," I said casually. "Come eat with me."

She hesitated. "I can't, Wesley. They charge me here. And right now, I just can't afford it."

I was surprised, maybe even a little angry on her behalf. I told her to wait and marched straight into the manager's office like I owned the place. I was greeted with a smile; they knew me well. I explained the situation and asked why Elisabeth was being charged. A few frowns, a few sighs, and then, with my best diplomatic tone and raised eyebrow, I got the answer I wanted.

"She'll eat here for free from now on," they said.

I returned to Elisabeth with a grin. "Sorted."

She looked at me in disbelief, both grateful and a little stunned.

"I can't believe how you operate," she said.

I smiled. "It's all about relationships. We live here. This isn't a job, it's a community. And when you respect the people around you, they respect you back."

That evening marked the start of a truly meaningful friendship. We began spending more time together, quiet coffees, late-night walks, shared stories. Looking back, there was probably more there. All the ingredients for something far deeper and romantic for sure. But we were both in long-distance relationships, and sometimes you don't see what's right in front of you until years later when you have the knowledge and experience to look back and say, "oh damn I missed that!".

Still, I remember her vividly. And I always will, I expect she is married, family and living in Germany or maybe still in Spain I will never know, unfortunately I am not great with names, and forgot her last name so that in short is the end of any chance of ever finding what became of her, a regret of being too young and care free to realise the importance of those small details.

A Celebration and a Lovely Evening

On the evening of 26 June 1992, Elisabeth surprised me by leaving a message at the Altura Park reception. It was her day off, and she wanted to meet up, a casual evening out, just the two of us. I got the note mid-afternoon and without hesitation, hopped onto my little red moped and zipped over to her staff housing tucked in the back of Santa Susanna. She wasn't in, so I left a handwritten note through her door: "6:30 PM at the

Altura Park — dinner on me, then maybe Mammas and Pappas after?"

The hours seemed to crawl after that. I got myself ready like it was something special, and in hindsight, maybe it was. I pulled out the iron I'd brought all the way from England (alongside my typewriter and surfboard, naturally, all the essentials for a rep), pressed my best trousers, and chose a clean shirt.

As I waited in reception, the receptionist glanced up from her desk and grinned. "Te ves muy guapo!" she called out — you look very handsome. I chuckled, slightly flustered, and gave her a wave.

Then Elisabeth arrived.

Her hair was down, not tied back like usual, cascading in black curls over her shoulders and her eyes were a lovely blue. She wore a sleek black leather jacket, white trousers, and a soft white blouse. She looked stunning with her tan, effortless, elegant. She kissed me on the cheek and gave me a hug, and we headed into the restaurant.

The moment we entered, the staff took notice. Waiters exchanged glances, the chef peeked from behind the kitchen door, and the head waiter himself came to serve us. They were clearly convinced they were witnessing the start of a romantic tale. Looking back, maybe they weren't wrong, or maybe we were just too caught up in our own professional distractions to realise what was there.

Dinner was lovely. We chatted like old friends, shared jokes, and exchanged stories that didn't involve hotel complaints or lost luggage. There was something refreshing about it, real conversation, easy company.

After dinner, we took a gentle walk through the town, then made our way to Mammas and Pappas, a charming little bar around the corner. That night, Denmark was playing Germany in the EURO 1992 Final, and the match flickered across a small TV in the background.

But the game wasn't the point.

We played pool, laughed loudly, and sipped local drinks while the bar buzzed around us. The décor was pure rustic charm, bamboo cladding, dark wood panelling, a thick haze of cigarette smoke curling through the ceiling fans. A few tourists were there, mostly from a local camping site, but otherwise the clientele was made up of ex-pats who had long ago made this place their new home.

Denmark ended up winning the match, but neither of us seemed to care much. The real victory was the company — two reps from different countries, unwinding in a tucked-away bar, far from the pressures of guest and arrival transfers.

As we walked back to the hotel, I walked her to her car. We shared a long goodbye, and as she drove off, I wandered back inside, feeling content.

At the front door, the night security guard was on duty. He grinned knowingly and, with a chuckle, called out, "Casanova!"

I laughed it off. "No, no," I said. "We're just friends."

But he didn't believe a word of it. In his mind, I was now the hotel's resident English gigolo — a title that, while ridiculous, would bring unexpected consequences down the line.

At the time, though, I just smiled and shook my head. Because that evening, whatever it was or wasn't, felt a little bit magical.

A Simple Escape

Every now and then, the days lined up just right, no emergencies, no transfers, no lost passports or panicked coach drivers. Just a still, golden day, where the world slowed down and offered you a little piece of peace.

One such day came in early June.

I had the morning free, and rather than sleep in or hang around the hotel, I decided to head inland, just for a few hours. I'd heard from one of the local waiters about a small village market up in the hills near Tordera, and something about the way he described it, shady plane trees, slow café terraces, fresh fruit laid out like jewels, stuck in my mind.

The sun had already warmed the pavement by the time I left the hotel. I threw a light shirt over my shoulders, packed a small bag with my notebook, a camera, and a bottle of water, and hopped onto my trusted red moped. The route to Tordera felt familiar, but that morning, it felt different, like I wasn't just travelling, I was escaping.

The road wound gently through the countryside, past fields of waving sunflowers and groves of silver-green olive trees. The sound of cicadas filled the air, and now and then I caught glimpses of farmhouses tucked into the hillsides, there terracotta roofs glowing in the sun. I passed old stone walls, roadside shrines, and glimpses of goats and donkeys wandering near the edge of the road. It was quiet, peacefully so, and the breeze against my face reminded me that not all joy comes from adrenaline. Some of it is found in the in-between.

The village market was exactly as I'd hoped, intimate, authentic, and brimming with colour. The square was shaded by wide plane trees, there bark like puzzle pieces, peeling and warm.

Stalls overflowed with plump peaches, bright red cherries, home-bottled olives, fresh-cut flowers, cheeses wrapped in cloth, and freshly baked breads still warm to the touch. Elderly women with woven baskets haggled over prices, and a man with a greying beard played a slow Catalan tune on a guitar leaning against a wall.

I bought a small basket of peaches, a wedge of goat cheese, a baguette, and a cold bottle of sparkling lemonade, and wandered to a bench under one of the old trees. I sat there watching the dance of village life, children chasing each other around the fountain, an old man playing dominos with a friend, and a couple lazily reading a newspaper, completely unbothered by time.

Later, I walked down to the riverbank, where the water flowed shallow and clear over smooth stones. I found a quiet spot in the shade, lay on the grass, and let the stillness wash over me. A dragonfly hovered over the water. Birds chirped in the distance. I took out my notebook and scribbled a few thoughts, nothing poetic, just fragments of contentment. The kind of peace you only realise you needed once you feel it.

I must have drifted off because when I opened my eyes, the sun had shifted. It was early afternoon, and a light breeze had picked up. I walked slowly back to the village, bought a small bottle of local honey as a souvenir, and rode back toward Pineda with the hills behind me and the coast in front.

That evening, as I returned to the usual rush, the hotel lobby noise, the reps' radio chatter (gossip about other things between companies), the constant ticking of the day's schedule, I felt different. Lighter. Clearer. Not everything needed to be fast or full. That day had reminded me of the value of slowness, of simplicity.

And sometimes, in a summer full of big stories and louder moments, it was the quiet days like this that stayed with you the longest.

A Night Out to Remember — or Not...

It was mid-summer when I found myself, once again, passing by Sergi's surf shop. He waved me over with his usual grin and booming voice.

"Pop by tonight — we're going out clubbing," he said. "It'll be a late one."

"What time?" I asked.

"Anytime!"

Well, I was British, we like a little more structure. So, I did the logical thing, had an early dinner, got myself ready, and walked down to the shop around 7 PM. Sergi lived above the surf shop with his family, so I knocked on the front door. His mum opened it, smiling warmly.

"Hola señora," I said. "He venido por Sergi."

"Sí, sí, entra, entra i seu," she replied, waving me in and motioning for me to sit.

What I quickly realised was that Sergi was nowhere to be found — not in the surf shop, not at home, not nearby. But his parents brought me in anyway, offered me a seat, and returned to watching their television show.

Despite the language barrier — they spoke Catalan, I spoke basic Spanish — they treated me like one of their own. After a while, his mum brought out pa amb tomàquet, the classic

Catalan tapa made with toasted bread, garlic, tomato, and olive oil. It was delicious. Sergi's father poured me a drink, and we sat there watching the news, occasionally exchanging broken phrases and sharing a laugh. Somehow, it worked.

By the time Sergi finally arrived at 9 PM, I was already half adopted by his family. This was the beginning of something wonderful, in the weeks that followed, I would stop by often. Sitting with his parents became my immersion course into Catalan culture and language. We built a friendship without the need for fluency — just consistency, kindness, and food.

But that evening wasn't meant to be quiet.

When Sergi arrived, Bruno and Mateo were with him. Sergi's voice, always unmistakable, could probably be heard from the street below. "Let's go," he said. "Tonight begins now."

As we piled into Bruno's car, I asked where we were off to.

"El Toro," Bruno said. "It's a locals' bar. You'll like it."

We drove into the old part of town, parked near a small square, and approached the bar. It had dark wooden doors, weathered signs, and no indication it was open to tourists. As we reached the entrance, the lads motioned for me to go in first.

Inside, the air was thick with smoke and low chatter. I stepped up to the bar.

The bartender looked me up and down.

"German or English?" he asked.

"English," I replied.

He narrowed his eyes. "No tourists here. Locals only."

There was a pause... then laughter exploded behind me. The lads burst in, arms around me, shouting in Catalan that I was family, that I lived here.

"Ahhhh, Casanova!" someone shouted from the back of the bar.

That name again.

Apparently, my beachside escapades with the Czech girls had spread, and I was now some kind of minor legend in their circle. Even in this tight-knit, tourist-free zone, I was welcomed, not for being English, but because of who I was with.

We moved out to the terraced garden at the back, where a large round table was filled with local friends of the lads, mostly single, all ready for a night out. Sergi ordered a round of drinks: local fruit-flavoured schnapps that looked innocent enough.

"Apple, peach... take your pick," he said with a grin.

I downed one, then another.

"How many do people usually drink?" I asked.

Bruno shrugged. "Ten? Fifteen maybe. You're fine."

So, I had twelve. Possibly more.

The next few hours were a blur of conversation, laughter, and flirtation. Two Spanish girls seemed especially interested in me, asking about England and sharing their dreams, one even mentioned planning to study in the UK the following year.

But then... I stood up.

And the world spun.

The last clear thing I remember is trying, for some absurd reason — to climb over a trellis fence instead of walking to the car. I vaguely recall Bruno shouting, "What are you doing?!"... The next memory: I'm in the back of the car, Bruno driving, and Mateo already having gone ahead with some of the others.

"Are you alright back there?" Bruno asked.

"Yeah, I'm surfing man...," I mumbled, completely out of it.

We arrived at the nightclub, lights flashing, music pounding. I vaguely remember the buzz of bodies, the beat of dance music, and what can only be described as a military operation of flirtation.

Locals, guys and girls, were meticulously prepping themselves in the bathroom, selecting their targets from the freshly arrived holidaymakers, and setting off to secure there "summer romances."

Mateo was a master of it. Smooth, confident, magnetic. I had to admire it — but it wasn't my game. Sure, a few girls approached me, but I politely declined. I was in a relationship, and besides, I had a job to protect. I was just intrigued to be on the opposite side of a holiday experience, and it was like a meat market!

What I don't remember is leaving the club... or getting home.

I woke up the next day in my bed, fully naked, and not the faintest clue how I'd got there.

All I knew was that it had been a night to remember — even if most of it had been lost to the Catalan schnapps and the swirl of summer madness.

A Ride to Blanes

Sometimes, when the rhythm of Pineda de Mar, calm though it usually was, began to feel a little to repetitive, I would hop on my little red moped and ride out to reset my mind. Pineda was never frantic like Lloret de Mar or Calella, but even the stillness had a way of pressing in after long days filled with timetables, meetings, and smiling until your cheeks ached.

On one warm, quiet morning, I decided to take a ride down to Blanes, a town I'd first visited with my parents years before. It held a special place in my heart. Blanes had a slightly more traditional, time-worn charm, the kind of town that felt steeped in Catalan roots, where things moved slowly, and the sea always seemed to be humming in the background.

I zipped along the coast road, the Mediterranean glinting to my right and the scent of wild herbs and sea salt drifting on the breeze. It was early enough that the sun was still soft, casting long shadows over the hillsides as I rolled through the gentle bends toward Blanes.

My first stop was the Mercat de la Fruita, the local fruit market. It was alive with gentle, easy energy, locals chatting in Catalan, baskets brimming with sun-warmed produce, the scent of peaches, melons, and garlic wafting through the air. I wandered slowly between the stalls, picking up a few peaches, a chunk of Manchego cheese, and a bottle of local fruit juice, all handed over with the kind of warm, knowing smiles that only come from small-town vendors who know their regulars, or spot a newcomer with a decent accent and good manners.

From there, I rode up the winding hill to the Botanical Garden, one of my favourite places along the coast. Perched high above the sea, the gardens overlooked the vast blue expanse of the

Mediterranean. I remembered coming here as a teenager, my dad pointing out the cactus terraces while my mum admired the flowers and archways. It hadn't changed much.

The paths were quiet that day, just a handful of visitors, the occasional rustle of a bird in the trees, and the soft buzz of insects dancing in the heat. I wandered through the garden slowly, letting my thoughts drift. I sat for a long while on a bench near the cliff edge, the waves crashing softly on the rocks below, the smell of salt and pine thick in the air.

I pulled out my peaches and Manchego, nibbling slowly as I watched a small boat cross the water far beneath me. It was one of those perfect, reflective moments, no noise, no rush, just the comfort of a full stomach and a wide view.

Eventually, I headed back down into town and lingered a little longer, a coffee at a small café, a walk along the promenade, and then back on the moped for the return to Pineda. As I rode home, the wind in my face and the late afternoon sun behind me, I felt lighter. Not just rested, realigned. When I returned to the Altura Park, one of the waiters saw me strolling in, bottle of juice under one arm.

"Where have you been, Wes?"

"Blanes," I said with a grin.

"Ah, tranquilo," he nodded, knowingly.

Exactly. Tranquil. That was the beauty of it. And as I headed to my room, still with the taste of peaches in my mouth and the sea air clinging to my clothes, I knew it had been the right decision. Not every day had to be exciting. Some were just quietly perfect.

Nightclub in Barcelona

One evening, Sergi approached me with a different kind of plan, no beach bar or rustic local haunt this time.

"We're going out to a special nightclub event in Barcelona," he told me. "Dress smart — really smart."

Later that evening, the legendary pink Seat Panda rolled up outside the hotel with Sergi and Bruno inside. Dressed to the nines, or at least as close as we could manage, we were ready for the 50-minute drive down the coast to the bright lights of Barcelona.

The atmosphere changed as we neared the city. The highway gave way to wide boulevards and grand architecture. Barcelona at night in 1992, just weeks before the Olympic Games, was electric, floodlit fountains, banners lining the streets, and the kind of palpable energy that only comes from a city poised on the edge of something monumental. As we drove through the city centre, I was struck by the contrast to Pineda. This was a different world.

We turned onto a boulevard where the traffic slowed. One look was enough to tell me this wasn't just any party. Ferraris, Porsches, Bentleys, and a few Rolls-Royces lined the street. Outside the venue, small clusters of people stood chatting, women in elegant evening dresses, men in tailored suits, polished shoes gleaming under streetlamps. The very best of Catalan society had clearly turned out.

Bruno glanced at our bubble-gum-coloured Panda and muttered, "Let's park around the corner. This beast would be a bit to noticeable out front."

Fair play.

The club itself was small and discreet, set back off the street with a subtle entrance and velvet ropes. Inside, it was a different universe, luxurious, elegant, softly lit with gold tones and sleek design. The music pulsed gently beneath the sound of polite conversation and clinking glasses. The air smelled of expensive perfume and cigars.

I had dressed well, cufflinks, a double-cuffed shirt, smart chinos, and a navy blazer with brass buttons. I felt like I belonged. Not because I was wealthy or part of this world, but because I'd learned something important about social spaces: people love to talk about themselves, and all you have to do is listen.

So, I did.

I mingled and observed, spoke with entrepreneurs, restaurateurs, boutique owners, hoteliers each with their own stories, ambitions, and insights. It was, I now realise, probably my first real networking event. I didn't push myself into conversations, I just asked the right questions and soaked it all in.

Sergi, meanwhile, worked the room like a seasoned professional. I learned that night that his surf shop was just one slice of his life — he also ran a ceramic tile factory, and was deep in conversations about trade, distribution, and partnerships. This was business Sergi — not beach Sergi. And I admired the seamless way he moved between worlds, something that I now do myself, and I can very much associate with this ability to live in different worlds.

Bruno, on the other hand, stuck out a little — bushy-haired, casual, the soul of the beach. He'd made an effort — polished shoes, shirt tucked in — but his essence was untameable. He still found himself laughing loudly at moments that didn't quite land in that refined setting. But somehow, even that made him endearing.

Barcelona's coastline, even at night, was something to behold. From the balcony at the club, we could see the glimmer of lights along the edge of the Port Vell, the glistening curve of the Mediterranean, and silhouettes of boats rocking gently in the dark. It was hard to believe this was just down the road from our sleepy little resort town. The contrast was beautiful.

We didn't stay too late. The night didn't end with raucous dancing or lost memories. It ended quietly, a peaceful drive home, the windows down, the sea breeze cooling our skin. The Panda buzzed along the coast road, and for once, none of us spoke much. We just soaked in the stillness of the early hours and the soft glow of a night well lived.

That night reminded me that Spain wasn't just sun, sand, and surfboards. It had layers, culture, sophistication, and ambition. And I was grateful to have seen a glimpse of it through the eyes of my Catalan friends.

That evening in Barcelona closed another chapter in my summer — one of many unforgettable nights, but unlike the rest, touched with elegance and the quiet thrill of stepping into a world I hadn't expected to find. A night out, yes — but also a moment of perspective. And with that, the days and nights of Pineda marched on, each one shaping a summer that was beginning to feel like a lifetime lived in miniature.

Chapter Six

It starts with a single word.

Not the kind printed in phrasebooks or drilled into your head by schoolteachers, but the kind you hear on a warm breeze, shouted between market stalls, whispered over a café table, or wrapped in laughter under the stars.

At first, language felt like background noise, a blur of syllables and gestures, like the radio tuned just off station before the days of digital radio when you were forced to select carefully the number on the dial. But somewhere along the way, those sounds began to stick. A "bon dia" here, a "vale" there, the ever useful "no pasa nada" when things inevitably went sideways.

Language wasn't something I studied. Well I did French at school and loved it but my school teacher left for another job in my third year at Sir William Nottidge school in Whitstable, a normal comprehensive school and despite being top group we lost our teacher and that was it, the replacement of the head teacher Mrs Hughes well was not of the same calibre and frankly I lost interest so did the majority of the class, she just never turned up for lessons, and we had cover teachers.

Language I found was something I absorbed, through repetition, mistakes, and the kindness of those who were patient enough to teach me without even realising it. Sergi's mother, with her plates of pa amb tomàquet. The hotel staff, slipping Catalan phrases into casual greetings. The coach drivers on the transfer coach journeys to collect our customers, who swore beautifully when traffic went bad and taught me to do the same.

My life that summer was written between languages, English, Spanish, Catalan, and a kind of universal language made of hand gestures, raised eyebrows, and the ever-dependable British grin. I became fluent in body language, in tone, in context. And over time, the words came to.

But this chapter isn't just about learning to say things. It's about learning to understand, really understand. What people mean when they don't have the right words. What lies between the sentences. What's carried in silence.

Because that's the thing about life abroad; you begin by trying to translate everything into your own terms… and then one day, without even noticing, you start seeing the world through theirs.

Some of the most meaningful connections I made that summer of 1992 came not from shared language, but from shared humanity. I'd sit at a table with Catalan friends, the conversation rolling on around me, some of it lost in translation, but never the feeling. Laughter didn't need subtitles. Neither did kindness.

As my vocabulary grew, so did my perspective. I realised how rich a culture becomes when you stop hearing it only in English. How identity, humour, and even emotion shift slightly when spoken in another tongue. Spanish had it's rhythm, bold, passionate, expressive. Catalan was different: lyrical, intimate, full of pride and nuance.

That summer, I didn't just learn how to speak. I learned how to listen.

Each morning, I'd be greeted, loudly and enthusiastically, by the voices from above. The hotel maids, who lived in the rooms just above mine, were early risers and made no secret of it. Originally from the Costa del Sol, they had travelled north to Costa Brava to work the summer season. Every morning, without fail, they would lean out their window and shout down to me with a chorus of "Hola, Hola Wesley!"

At first, it was amusing. Then it became routine. Eventually, it became a kind of affection. Over time, the greetings turned into longer exchanges. The occasional flirtatious line made its way in to, especially on evenings when they'd had a little sangria. One of their favourites, screamed out the window, followed by fits of giggles, was "Hola Wesley, quickie quickie por favour!" It was cheeky, playful, and undeniably hilarious.

Joking aside, they were a brilliant bunch, warm, hardworking women with huge personalities and endless energy. At times, I'll admit I grew tired of hearing the word "Hola" everywhere I turned. I used to think, why can't they just say "hi" or even "ciao" like the Italians? But "hola" it was, and eventually I embraced it like everything else.

One evening, they invited me to join them for a night out. This sort of thing was often frowned upon by some of the more traditionally minded reps. I remember one in particular from another company who scowled at me and asked, "Why would you mix with the hotel staff when the guests are far better options?"

To me, the answer was simple. I wasn't there to chase fleeting flings with holidaymakers. I was there to live in Spain, to be part of it. And that meant living among the locals, learning their rhythms, understanding their world. I've always carried that mindset, wherever I go, I do my best to live like a local.

So, of course, I agreed. Five lively Spanish women asking me to go out with them? Why on earth would I say no?

They didn't have much in the way of material wealth, but they had heart. They were proud, joyful, and carried a kind of resilience that I admired. That night, we headed to a local nightclub, the kind of place they only visited once every few weeks. there English was limited. My Spanish was still patchy at best. Conversations were comical at times, a mashup of facial expressions, guessing games, and the occasional burst of unexpected understanding.

To add to my own embarrassment, I'd made a questionable outfit choice, a blue blazer and grey slack trousers. Not normally a problem, except under the harsh ultraviolet club lights it revealed a slight dusting of dandruff like fresh snow on a ski slope. After a quick wardrobe adjustment, I relaxed a bit more and leaned into the experience.

We danced, we laughed, we shouted broken phrases across the table. And somewhere in the blur of music and shared smiles, I realised I was picking up more than just vocabulary. I was learning about culture, how different even one part of Spain could be from another. I had worked across Spanish resorts with Thomson Holidays before, but these girls showed me something new, a slice of southern Spanish warmth, blended into the Catalan north, creating a culture all its own.

I left that night with a few new words, a few new memories, and a deeper appreciation for the people who surrounded me. Language, it turns out, is never just about grammar — it's about connection. And some of the best conversations I had that summer didn't need perfect sentences, they just needed openness, patience, and a little bit of laughter.

One afternoon, in late May, I found myself with a rare few hours of total stillness. No airport runs, no excursion pickups, no complaints about broken air conditioning or missed wake-up calls. The heat hung lazily in the air, and the streets of Pineda were quiet, half-asleep under the afternoon sun.

I wandered into the main small, shaded square just behind the main tourist drag, a place I hadn't spent much time before. A row of locals sat on a bench beneath an old sycamore tree, fanning themselves, sharing slow conversation. There was a little bar tucked in the corner, it's door wide open, letting the breeze carry the smell of ground coffee and grilled prawns into the square.

Inside, a man in his sixties stood behind the bar, humming a Catalan tune I didn't know but somehow recognised. I ordered a café con leche and sat outside, watching the rhythm of the street unfold; the gentle clink of spoons in cups, the rustle of a newspaper turning, the occasional bark of a far-off dog. It was like life was whispering instead of speaking.

After a while, the barman came out with a drink of his own and sat down at the table next to me. He looked over, smiled, and said something I only half understood.

"Calor així, només els grills tenen ganes de xerrar."

Something about the heat and crickets wanting to talk — that was all I caught. But I smiled anyway and replied, in my best Catalan, "Sí… és un dia tranquil."

He laughed, not unkindly, and began to speak slower, clearer. We ended up talking for nearly an hour, in a mix of Catalan, Spanish, and occasionally English. He told me about the square, how it had been his father's favourite place to sit. About the changes he'd seen since tourism had arrived. About the times he'd spent visiting London as a young man, when he was trying to learn English.

We were two strangers from different countries, different generations, and yet, through that shared dance of language, broken, imperfect, human, we connected.

Before I left, he handed me a folded napkin with a phrase written on it: "No tothom que parla, escolta. Però tu escoltes bé."

Not everyone who speaks, listens. But you listen well.

I kept that napkin in my wallet for years.

Because that, in the end, is what learning a language abroad gave me, not just words, but ways to see, ways to understand, and a new kind of quiet confidence that comes from knowing you can build a bridge out of even the most fragile syllables.

From that quiet afternoon in the square, something shifted in me.

I found myself returning there in the evenings, drawn not by obligation or boredom, but by the feeling that I'd tapped into something real, something timeless. As the sun began to lower and the sticky heat of the day gave way to a cooler breeze, the square would slowly fill with people.

Mostly older Catalan residents, some in crisp linen, others in softly faded dresses or pressed trousers, would emerge from shaded alleyways and nearby buildings. They'd gather quietly at first, exchanging nods and smiles. Then, from the far corner of the square, the music would start. A soft accordion, a tamborí drum, sometimes even a flabiol flute. And just like that, the dancing began.

It was the Sardana, the traditional Catalan circle dance, a symbol of unity, of defiance, of cultural pride. Men and women, young and old, would form circles hand-in-hand. there arms raised, fingers lightly interlaced, they moved in precise, graceful steps, there feet weaving back and forth in quiet synchrony.

At first, I simply watched. I'd lean against one of the local big trees in the square, peach juice still on my fingers from a nearby market stall, and take it all in. The elegance of it. The warmth. The unspoken history that pulsed through each step and note.

Then, one evening, a woman of perhaps sixty or seventy, silver hair pinned neatly, wearing soft espadrilles and a bright smile, looked over at me and extended her hand.

"Vols ballar?"

I hesitated for a moment, then smiled and stepped into the circle.

From that night on, I danced. Not every night, but enough to be recognised. Enough to become a familiar face among the rhythm and steps. Enough that the locals began to nod to me as I arrived, not as an outsider, but as someone trying. Someone who wasn't just passing through with a clipboard and a resort badge, but someone who wanted to belong.

It was one of the most quietly beautiful honours of that summer, not a promotion, not a bonus, not even a compliment. It was acceptance.

No other rep in the resort, at least none that I knew, had ever spoken of these moments. They were more likely to be found queuing up outside the tourist-heavy nightclubs in Lloret de Mar or diving into cheap sangria and neon-lit karaoke. I wasn't judging that life was theirs to live. But mine was different.

Elizabeth, my German overseas representative friend from the Altura Park, was the only one I knew who shared a similar pull toward local culture. She too would skip the big nights out for something more grounded, a dinner with hotel staff, a stroll through town, or quiet conversation at a tucked-away café. Maybe that's why we connected so well.

But for me, it was these evenings in the square, the laughter, the slow turns, the stories told in steps rather than sentences, that made me feel most at home.

In the heart of Catalonia, among strangers who became acquaintances and moments that became memories, I stopped feeling like a guest.

I was living in Spain.
And Spain, somehow, was living in me.

But of course, learning a language, or in this case, two, wasn't always poetic. In fact, the first few weeks of trying to understand the difference between Spanish and Catalan were more confusing than enlightening.

Catalan, to the untrained ear, can sound like a mix of French, Spanish, and someone clearing their throat, all at once. I'd walk into a café feeling confident with a freshly rehearsed Spanish phrase, only to be met with a reply in Catalan that sounded nothing like what I'd just said. I'd stare, nod politely, and say "sí", which occasionally resulted in ordering things I definitely hadn't meant to. Once I thought I was asking for a small orange juice and ended up with a plate of grilled aubergines. I ate them. Out of politeness. Sort of.

The locals were kind, though. Amused, but kind. Sergi once told me Catalan was like "Spanish with pride" and that felt about right. It wasn't just a dialect. It was a statement. A culture. And I was determined to respect it, even if I occasionally butchered it.

That summer I learned that "adéu" wasn't just goodbye, it was how you signed off a conversation with trust. That "molt bé" wasn't just "very good," it was a way of saying, you're doing just fine. And I also learned never to confuse "embolicar" (to wrap something) with "embolic" (a mess or complication) when asking about laundry at the hotel. That caused a few red faces in the staff room.

But my connection to Catalan started long before I stepped foot in Pineda de Mar, though I didn't realise it at the time.

As a boy, on one of my very first family holidays to Spain, I wandered down a narrow backstreet in a quiet Catalan coastal town and found myself in one of those charming little tourist shops that sold everything from wooden castanets to flamenco dolls and fridge magnets. Among the clutter, hanging slightly crooked on the back wall, was a small Catalan sign.

It showed a cartoon image of an old man grinning while sitting on a toilet, and above him, in big bold lettering, was a phrase written entirely in Catalan. I had no idea what it meant, and neither did my parents, but something about the look of it made me laugh, so I bought it with my own pocket money.

That sign went straight onto the back of the toilet door back home in Whitstable, where it remained for years. A little piece of mystery Catalonia in Kent. Every family member, guest, or plumber who visited would inevitably ask, "What does it mean?" And the answer was always the same: "No idea."

It wasn't until seven years later, when I was working at Thomson Holidays, that someone fluent in Catalan finally translated it for me.

It read: "A wise man says what a wise man does, but a wise man does what a wise man says."

I laughed for days. All that time, it had been quietly offering up a little nugget of wisdom, right there, in the loo.

And I suppose, in a roundabout way, that little wooden plaque planted something in me. A curiosity. A seed of connection to a language and culture I wouldn't come to truly understand until that summer of '92.

Funny how life works like that. One minute you're giggling at a toilet sign, and the next you're living in a town where the words finally start to make sense.

So much of that summer was about learning to speak. But even more of it was about learning to listen, to words, to people, to cultures that weren't mine, but somehow let me in anyway.

Whether it was dancing in a circle beneath the setting sun, sharing laughter in a language I barely understood, or slowly unlocking the meaning behind an old sign I'd bought as a boy, the message was always the same:

Language isn't just how we speak. It's how we connect.

And somewhere between the "holas" shouted down from the hotel windows, the slow turning of the Sardana in the square, and the broken conversations over pa amb tomàquet and peach schnapps, I stopped being just a guest in Spain. I had, at last, become part of its rhythm.

Chapter Seven

The summer of 1992 arrived not with a bang, but with a kind of growing hum, like a kettle slowly coming to the boil. You could feel it rising through the streets of Catalonia, seeping in through the windows of cafés, and bars and echoing across the tiled rooftops of sleepy coastal towns.

Even in quieter corners like Pineda de Mar, there was a sense that something bigger was stirring, something historical. Barcelona, just up the coast on the train, was being polished like a diamond. Roads were being resurfaced, railways sharpened, fountains refilled, and banners stretched between lampposts with pride. Spain was preparing to host the world.

The 1992 Summer Olympics weren't just a sporting event, they were a moment of transformation. A country once defined by its past was suddenly stepping boldly into the future, and you could feel that optimism in the air.

For those of us living and working in the region, it was more than headlines or flag-waving. It was in the details, the trains running just a bit more on time, the burst of new languages from arriving guests, the unusual sharpness in hotel uniforms, as if the country itself had straightened it's collar and was finally ready for its close-up.

What I found particularly fascinating that summer was the sudden emergence of a specialist sports tour operator from the UK, one that had seemingly taken over the coast. They weren't just bringing your average holidaymakers, they were hosting families of athletes, relatives, sponsors, and fans who had travelled to Spain specifically for the Olympic Games.

Cosmos Holidays had its usual mix of families and travellers to, of course, but this other company had organised things on a whole different scale. Thousands of people. All wrapped in white, literally, as they'd issued matching clothing that made them instantly recognisable wherever they went. It became something of a running visual gag, every morning, like clockwork, you could look out from the hotel breakfast terrace and see a long procession of white-clad guests marching like a silent parade along the seafront promenade, heading for Pineda's train station.

They were off to Barcelona, of course, the journey taking about an hour and fifteen minutes each way on the local train, which terminated at Estació de Sants, Barcelona's main railway station. From there, specialist transfers were waiting to ferry them to venues scattered across the city: gymnastics in one place, archery in another, volleyball on the beach. It was a logistical dance, and watching it play out each day from the edge of a sleepy coastal town felt oddly surreal.

Before the Games officially began, our excursion programme even included a sneak peek at the Olympic Village, a driving tour through the newly constructed athlete housing, set high above the city. The coach would wind its way into the hills, passengers peering out in awe as the guide detailed the architectural ambition of it all. It was one of our most popular trips. Funny thing is… I never actually went on it myself. There just wasn't the time. The season was relentless, and I was being pulled in every direction by guests, duties, transfers, and daily dramas.

But it was during this hectic Olympic period that I made one of the more embarrassing slip-ups of my travel career. It was a coach transfer, a standard run, and I was doing my usual welcome speech, probably on autopilot if I'm being honest. I'd seen so many of these "Olympic crowd" groups over the weeks, all walking in long lines in there matching whites, and in a moment of unfiltered foolishness, I made a sarcastic joke over the microphone about them.

I think I said something along the lines of: "If you're wondering who those people are all walking in formation dressed in white every morning — don't worry, it's not a cult, just the proud parents of future Olympians living off their kids' glory…"

Then, as if to cover myself with misplaced confidence, I added, "Unless anyone here's connected to the Olympics?" — fully expecting silence.

Instead, six hands went up.
I froze.

Instant regret. I felt like such a muppet.

I spent the rest of the coach ride mentally kicking myself, and afterward, I made a point to personally apologise to each of them. They were gracious, thankfully, good-humoured even, but I learned a valuable lesson that day:

Never assume who's listening. Especially not in Olympic season.

It was that year, the Olympic year, that I truly started to get into the Games. Not just casually following the highlights but properly absorbed. Enthralled, even. I couldn't get enough of it. The excitement was infectious, and for the first time in my life, I was really pulled in, especially by the rowing.

There was something stirring about it all, the discipline, the teamwork, the grit, and I found myself completely invested in

Team GB's rowing campaign. I'd take my lunch breaks at the poolside café of the Altura Park Hotel, sat at a sun-bleached plastic table with a chilled glass of water and a half roast spit chicken with chips, salad, and always a good squirt of tomato ketchup on the side. You might scoff at the meal choice but trust me — that chicken was the business. It turned slowly on the spit outside all day, the smell drifting over the pool like a magnet.

The chef had become a mate by then. He'd always flash a grin when he saw me coming and carve me the best half, crispy skin and all. He'd laugh when I insisted on ketchup, probably thought it was a very British quirk, but he never judged. Always a good laugh, always welcoming.

So, there I'd be, plate balanced in front of me, and the TV perched up on a bracket in the corner of the café wall, slightly fuzzy reception but good enough. And when those races came on — Matthew Pinsent, Steve Redgrave, Garry Herbert, the Searle brothers — I'd be absolutely glued to it, cheering them on like I was in the stands. I remember sitting bolt upright, half a chip mid-air, as they crossed the line for gold. It was emotional. Genuinely so. I wasn't at the venue, but being just 50 minutes away, I felt close enough to be part of it. As if somehow, just living in Catalonia that summer made me part of the Olympic story to.

Now, I know some might raise an eyebrow at my lunch habit's. Spanish food was, and still is, one of my great loves. I had it daily, naturally. But once in a while, especially if I'd been running about all day and found myself near Lloret de Mar, I'd stop in at this Irish bar tucked off the main drag. Why? Because they did, without question, the best kidney, mash, peas and gravy I'd had outside of home. It was heaven.

The place was a proper expat haunt, during the day at least. In the evenings it filled with tourists after pints and football, but during the lunch hours it was the unofficial embassy of the British abroad. You had a plumber in the corner, a handyman playing darts, an estate agent flicking through the local paper, and someone else who "knew a bloke who could get you anything." It was like a local parish council meeting with pints.

I remember chatting to the owner Janet, one day, and she said, "Wesley, honestly mate, you don't even need to speak Spanish here — everything's covered!"

And weirdly, she wasn't wrong. That tiny bar had its own ecosystem. You needed a boiler fixed? Sorted. A flat painted? Give Jim a ring. Somewhere to watch the Grand National with people who missed Marmite. That was your place.

It was an odd contrast, on the one hand I was doing everything I could to immerse myself in Spanish life, Catalan culture, local traditions. On the other, just up the road, was this pocket of Britain that hadn't moved on since 1978. And yet, both worlds existed side by side. And in their own way, both gave me something I needed that summer.

In fact, sometimes when I wasn't feeling well, those days when a dodgy stomach bug or the heat had worn me down, I'd get on my little red moped and head straight for Lloret de Mar. Not for a beach or a disco, but to that Irish bar for one thing; a proper English-style meal to settle my stomach. Technically speaking, of course, it was Spanish meat and veg, local produce, local hands, but it was cooked in a way that felt familiar. Mashed potatoes with a bit of Spanish flair. Gravy with a Mediterranean undertone. It wasn't quite home, but it was close enough, and when you're tired or under the weather abroad, sometimes close enough is all you need.

There was comfort in it, not just in the food, but in the atmosphere. It was a place that didn't ask questions, didn't need translations, didn't require you to be "on." Just walk in, nod to the lads, and tuck into a plate of something hearty.

It wasn't glamorous. It wasn't particularly Catalan. But it was part of my Spain that summer, and part of how I made it through.

One afternoon in mid-July, just as the Olympic buzz had really hit full stride, I was walking through Pineda's beachfront after finishing my rounds. It was hot, not just warm, but that thick kind of heat that made the pavement feel soft underfoot and the air smell of sea salt and melting sunscreen.

I stopped to grab a Fanta Limón from one of the small kiosks near the promenade and sat down on a bench overlooking the beach. I hadn't been there long when an older British gentleman, sunhat, socks with sandals, and a pair of Union Jack shorts I'll never unsee, shuffled over and asked if he could sit. I nodded, and we sat in silence for a few minutes, both watching the families trickle down to the sea.

Then he turned to me and said, "You don't mind me asking, young man, but do you work here or are you just one of those... tan professionals?"

I nearly choked on my Fanta.

I replied, "I work here actually. I'm a Cosmos holidays rep."

He raised an eyebrow. "Well, you don't look stressed enough to be a rep."

We got chatting, and it turned out he'd been in Barcelona the day before for the Olympics. Saw the athletics. Said the crowd roared like it was Wembley. He was here with his wife and her sister, though he admitted he was only half paying attention to the events, he was mostly in awe of the stadium sandwiches, which, he insisted, were "unreasonably good."

Before he left, he patted me on the shoulder and said, "Nice tan. Keep up the good work, sunshine. You're doing Her Majesty proud."

I never got his name. But I remember thinking, this is what the Olympics does, it brings together a sunburnt pensioner in novelty shorts, a young British rep, and somehow, in the haze of a golden Spanish afternoon, it all just made perfect sense.

Chapter Eight

It's strange how a place you've grown comfortable in can suddenly feel unfamiliar the moment someone new is about to step into it.

The morning air in Pineda de Mar was the same as always, warm, light, tinged with salt. The mopeds buzzed past, the cafes laid out their chairs, the beach was already beginning to stir with early risers and sunseekers. But for me, everything felt slightly… suspended. As if the world had taken a breath and was holding it in.

Lelena was on her way.

She was travelling by bus, of all things, a long and winding journey from Praha (Prague) to Barcelona, weaving through the heart of Europe. It would take the best part of a day and a half, if not more. She was making her way from her hometown in southern Bohemia, the fairytale-like town of Český Krumlov, where cobbled streets curled around a bend in the river, and where she lived a life so very different from the one I had here on the Catalan coast.

It had been weeks in the planning. Letters exchanged. Phone calls made from dark phone booths with dodgy connections and even dodgier international charges. And now the moment was nearly here, after all the promises and build-up, she was coming to me.

And I… I was pacing.

I kept checking my watch. Checking the time difference between Spain and the Czech Republic. Wondering whether the coach had left on time. Wondering if she'd made her connection. Wondering what she'd be thinking, looking out of the window as the miles passed under her.

There's a particular kind of anticipation when someone you care about is crossing borders to find you, it's not quite anxiety, not quite excitement, but something deeply human. A fusion of love, hope, and nerves, all bundled up in the knowledge that everything's about to change.

And it was.
I just didn't know how much yet.

The hotel management had a clear and unwavering policy: no girlfriends allowed in staff accommodation. At the time I thought it was a bit harsh, even a little unfair, but I could understand it. This was still Spain in the early '90s, a deeply Catholic country in many ways, and the hotel wanted to avoid any suggestion of impropriety, the management were strict on this. Still, I had a promise to keep.

You see, I'd given my word to Otto, Lelena's father, a former top pilot in the Czech Air Force, who had a presence that could straighten a room. I told him she'd have her own room, her own space, and no unnecessary nonsense. So, I'd arranged a quiet room for her just a few doors down from mine. The management approved it. She'd have peace and privacy. And I'd have the honour of a promise kept. The only downside was it would cost me nearly two months' salary, even with discount!

I also made sure to give a quiet word to the maids who lived above me, that lively, spirited lot from the Costa del Sol who had turned shouting down to me each morning into something of a ritual. Like clockwork, they'd lean out of their windows with big grins and belt out, "Hola, Wesley!" as if announcing the start of some grand fiesta. And if they were in particularly cheeky moods, they'd call out as previously mentioned, "Quickie, quickie por favour!" before dissolving into laughter. It was harmless fun, but with Lelena's arrival just days away, I thought it best to put a lid on it. I explained, as gently and diplomatically as I could, that my señorita was coming to stay and that a touch of discretion would go a long way. They grinned, winked, and gave me a thumbs up, loud and mischievous they may have been, but they were a loyal, warm-hearted bunch.

Across the hall from me lived one of the entertainers, a Dutch woman, tall, elegant, and with a kind of effortless beauty that made her the centre of attention wherever she went. Every man in the hotel seemed to be enamoured with her, except me. Not out of stubbornness, she just wasn't my type. Ironically, that's probably what made her start talking to me in the first place.

Our friendship began in an unusual way.

She'd had a massive fallout, with the hotel management, her male co-entertainer, and a group of rival company reps. It had all boiled over into shouting and tears. Later, I knocked on her door. She opened it, still visibly upset.

"You alright?" I asked gently.

"I'm fine," she said, a bit shaken. "Come in, if you like."

She had just stepped out of the shower, towel drying her hair, completely naked, which in true continental fashion didn't seem to faze her in the slightest. She strolled into the room without a second thought, chatting away. I followed, calmly, eyes focused above the shoulders like a proper gentleman, though it was hard not to notice, she was absolutely stunning, the kind of figure that made you understand why people wrote poetry.

And then she asked it.

"Do you like me?" she said. "I mean... like me like me?"

I smiled and said, "You're lovely, but no, I don't fancy you. I've got a girlfriend coming over. And more than that, I just don't see you that way."

She was quiet for a second — then grinned. "You're the first man here to say that."

I explained I'd come in because I heard she was upset, and I wanted to help. She opened up. Apparently, her male entertainer partner had been bad-mouthing her to management, spreading lies and turning others against her. She was being blamed for things she hadn't done, and the rival reps weren't exactly offering a shoulder to lean on.

"Well," I said, "leave it with me."

I walked down to the management office, sat down and laid it all out. Explained that Cosmos guests had raised complaints about the male entertainer, and that frankly, the best talent they had — this Dutch woman — was being mistreated and demoralised. The manager raised an eyebrow and said, "Wesley, you should go into politics. That was a tidy summary."

I smiled. "No politics. Just fairness. I'm not here to take sides — just to make sure the right things done."

From there, I made my way to the competitor reps' desk. They stood there smug, none the wiser about who I really was or where I'd come from. I calmly let them know there was now a formal complaint on record, and that they'd be wise to distance themselves from the male entertainer. I ended the conversation with a simple line: "And just so you're aware, I'll be passing this along to Charles Newbold in London, if it isn't resolved."

their faces changed. The name meant something — he was, after all, the CEO of Thomson Holidays. And what business did a Cosmos rep have knowing him?

They didn't know I'd been with Thomson before and knew all senior management well. They didn't know who I was. But they knew enough to back off.

Later that evening, I saw the Dutch entertainer in the corridor.

"It's sorted," I said. "Give it 24 hours. You'll see."

She stared at me, surprised. Something had shifted. She hadn't expected anyone to go to bat for her — especially not me.

From that day on, she started popping by more often. Sometimes half-dressed between shows, sometimes in a robe with her hair up. But never flirtatious, never suggestive, just genuine friendship. She told me she'd never felt so at ease around a man. That it was nice to be seen for more than her looks.

I told her the truth. "I've just never really fancied Dutch girls," I said with a grin. "No idea why."

She laughed and said, "Then lucky me, I finally found someone who didn't."

The Arrival…

I set off from Pineda de Mar early that afternoon, boarding the train that clattered and hummed it's way along the sun-soaked coastline. It was early August, the kind of day where the heat settles on your shoulders like a warm towel, hot, sticky, and unmistakably high summer. The train was packed with day-trippers from Barcelona, sun-pink and weary, heading back to the city after a few hours by the sea.

I always found it odd, to be honest, why so many came all the way up to Pineda when there were perfectly good beaches much closer to home — Castelldefels, Sitges, even Barceloneta itself had it's charm. Still, who was I to question where people found their pockets of peace?

The plan was straightforward. The Czech coach made this journey regularly in the summer months — long haul from Praha to Barcelona — and usually rolled in between 5 and 6 PM at the coach arrival bays near Sants Railway Station, just outside the main terminal. I'd been there before, so I knew where I was going. No guesswork.

I arrived in good time, gave myself a little window to stretch my legs, wander through the boulevards, admire the city's bold, blocky architecture and the odd flash of Gaudí in the distance. I found a shady bench near Parc de l'Espanya, had a small snack and a bottle of water, and let the moment settle. Today wasn't just about logistics, it was something more. Something I had looked forward to for weeks.

She was almost here.

As the hours rolled by, I wandered over to the coach drop-off point, just across the road from where I'd been sat earlier and had a good look about to see if anyone else was waiting. Nothing. No one. Just a quiet patch of concrete and the hum of the city in the background. So, I plonked myself down in the shade, leaned back, and did what we all did best in Spain: waited.

Minutes turned into half hours... half hours into hours... and before long, the clock had ticked well past the coach's expected arrival time. It was gone 7pm now. The heat had dropped a little, thankfully, but it had settled into that sticky, claggy sort of warmth that clings to your shirt and makes your socks feel like sandpaper. I was feeling uncomfortable, if I'm honest. A bit like a roast chicken left to rest in clingfilm.

Luckily, I'd been smart enough to arrange the next day off, so I wasn't in a total flap about the delay. What I was more worried about was the last train back to Pineda de Mar. I knew full well that the final one was due to leave at 9:10pm, and with the journey being a good hour and ten, if we missed that... well, the options were slim. Buses would be long gone. Taxis were out of the question; I wasn't made of pesetas (not Euros in the 1992).

9:00pm came and went. No coach. No girlfriend. No hope of catching the train.

But that wasn't the bit that had me twitching, what really started to eat at me was where on earth was the coach? That's a long way to be missing in action. Soon it was 10pm, and I was sat there in the dark, now watching the streetlamps flicker on, wondering if I'd been daft to come at all.

That's when a man appeared. Czech, I guessed straightaway, something about the way he dressed, the look on his face. Not touristy. Familiar. He walked over to the small signboard marking the coach arrival area, checked it over, and looked around with the same confused expression I'd probably had all evening.

I walked up and asked, "Do you speak English?"
And to my relief, he did. Quite well, actually.

Turned out he was a representative for the Czech bus company, here to meet the drivers and issue a new departure schedule for the return leg the following day. There'd been a technical fault — a breakdown somewhere en route. The coach was running again now, he explained, but it had been severely delayed. New arrival time? 4:00am. At the earliest.

And there it was. Four in the morning. I did a quick calculation in my head, if I called Sergi or Bruno and asked for a rescue run back to Pineda, I'd just about get three hours kip before needing to head back out again. Pointless. I didn't fancy dragging anyone out, and I knew there was only one reasonable choice.

I was going to sleep rough in Barcelona.

The bench outside the coach terminal would be my hotel for the night.

Still, before settling in for my glamorous bus stop pavement accommodation, I decided to pop back into the station café before it shut completely. I grabbed a coffee, something vaguely edible to nibble on, and a bottle of water for the long wait ahead.

Remember in those days we had No mobile phones. No updates. No internet. Just me, a bag, some lukewarm caffeine, and the hope that love was still somewhere on a coach coming down through France.

As the hours crawled by and the station grew quieter, I settled in on my bench, not exactly a four-star establishment, but I'd seen worse. I used my bag and jumper as a pillow, kept my valuables tucked close, and tried to relax under the faint orange glow of the streetlamps. Not ideal, but I'd made peace with it.

What I hadn't expected, though, was the regular visits from the local police.

Every thirty minutes, like clockwork, the same squad car would swing by headlights briefly blinding me as it rolled to a stop. Each time, the window would come down with a whirr, and the same officer would lean out and check in.

"¿Todo bien, chico?"
"All good, mate?" I'd nod, smile, and wave them on.

I'd explained to them earlier in the evening that I was an overseas rep, waiting for a coach from Czech Republic. I must have looked equal parts dodgy and pitiful, a young Brit with bags under his eyes, curled up on a bench with half a chicken sandwich and a bottle of water like a low-budget travel documentary.

To their credit, they were lovely. Proper decent local police. They offered to help, asked if I needed a lift, somewhere safer to wait, even suggested the little café down the road might still let me sit inside for a bit. But I was settled by that point, and stubborn, and I think in some odd way I wanted to see the night through, as if enduring it added something noble to the story.

At one point, around half two in the morning, the officer gave me a thumbs-up and a wink before driving off again, and I had to laugh. I'd become part of their overnight patrol routine. Not a threat. Not a problem. Just some daft Brit rep on a bench waiting for a coach — and somehow, that made me feel weirdly safe.

It wasn't glamorous, but it was... well, it was Spain. And I was living it, bench and all.

At 4:20 in the morning, just as the sky was beginning to shift from deep indigo to the faintest tinge of pale grey, I saw the coach turn the corner.

It's headlights swept across the pavement like a lighthouse beam, and the familiar logo on the side made my heart leap, not because of the coach itself, but because I knew she was finally here. After all the waiting, the wandering, the coffees, the nearly-dozing-off-then-being-woken-by-police patrols, the moment had arrived.

The coach eased its way to the kerb, air brakes hissing, engine ticking over. I stood up from my bench, dusted myself off a bit, tried to look semi-human, and waited anxiously as the passengers began to file off, stiff-legged, bleary-eyed, blinking into the pre-dawn gloom.

And then there she was.

Lelena.

Smiling. Sleepy. Slightly grumpy in that way you are when you've been on a coach for a small eternity, but still beautiful. Her blonde hair on her shoulders, and she looked around until her eyes found me.

She didn't say much, just gave me a half-smile and that little nod she always did, but that was enough. I stepped forward, took her bag from her without saying a word, and said with a grin, "Come on — let's get out of here."

We walked across to the main station, quietly, both of us tired, both of us knowing that the planned big, exciting first day together was quickly dissolving into something far more low key.

The first train to Pineda de Mar wasn't until 5:20am, so we had a bit of time to wait — again. But at least this time, we were waiting together.

I'll admit, I felt a small pang of disappointment. I'd built up the idea of this lovely day, a proper romantic start to her visit, full of sunshine, sights, and energy. But the reality was, we'd both need sleep. And after that, maybe just a gentle wander to the beach or a nap by the pool. The big plans could wait.

Because in the end, she was here. And sometimes, just showing up after a long, long journey is more than enough.

The Journey to Pineda…

The train pulled out of Barcelona Sants station just after 5:20 AM, it's wheels clicking rhythmically along the tracks like a metronome easing us into the dawn. The carriage was quiet, still washed in the grey tones of early morning. There were only a handful of other passengers, mostly early workers or groggy travellers, and the soft hum of the train was the only real sound.

I was tired, of course. Anyone would be. But truth be told, I was fine. As an overseas rep, you get used to strange hours and impossible timetables. Late transfers, last-minute changes, and long nights with no guarantee of sleep, it was all part of the job. I'd already managed 72 hours without a wink of sleep earlier that season, bouncing between hotels, sorting crises, and smiling through it all with the charm of a man running on adrenaline and blind optimism.

So, this? This was a breeze. Just a delay. Just a mild inconvenience with a nice sunrise on the horizon and my girlfriend finally by my side. I'd take that.

As the train crept beyond the edges of the city, Barcelona slowly began to blur behind us, the towering flats replaced by sleepy suburbs, still largely shuttered up, with only the odd café owner beginning to stir. Within minutes, the view transformed, and there it was, the Mediterranean Sea, stretching out beside us, calm and glassy under the soft blush of dawn.

It's hard to describe how perfect that stretch of coastline feels at that hour unless you've lived it. The train follows the shoreline so closely it's as if it's trying to keep the sea company. And that morning, the Mediterranean looked like silk, smooth, still, reflecting the light like a mirror laid flat on the earth.

We passed through Badalona, then Montgat, and Masnou — all of them still wiping the sleep from their eyes. You'd spot the odd dog walker pacing the promenade or a fisherman sat quietly on the rocks, line cast with hope. Beaches empty, waves gently lapping at the shore, and in the far distance, the first golden glow creeping up from behind the hills.

Every few stops the train would exhale with a sigh of brakes, the doors sliding open to almost no one. This wasn't the time for tourists or commuters yet. This was the time for ghosts and locals, for quiet and reflection.

I glanced over at Lelena, her head lightly resting against the window. She looked tired, of course, who wouldn't after that journey? But she was here. And watching her, I felt a strange mixture of pride and peace. We weren't talking much. We didn't need to. We were sharing something, a kind of unspoken agreement that this moment, this sleepy coastal train ride, was the start of a new chapter. And it didn't need words.

We passed through Vilassar, Mataró, then Arenys de Mar, each stop unfolding like pearls on a string, each little town hugging the coast with it's own sleepy rhythm. In some places, the beaches looked golden and smooth. In others, coarse and stony. But always, that calm, endless sea beside us. So familiar to me now, yet always just a little magical at this hour.

I sat there quietly, letting the sun slowly warm my legs through the glass, feeling the train rock gently beneath us, and realised I was doing something rare for a rep in the peak of season; I was still and calm.

As Calella came and went, and then Pineda de Mar finally approached, I started gathering my bit's. Bag, jacket, Lelena's bag. The station came into view, just as the sun finally crested the hills behind us, lighting the town in a soft, golden wash.

I nudged her gently.

"We're here," I said.

And we were.

Not just in Pineda. But in the start of whatever this part of the summer, and maybe something more, was going to become.

We stepped off the train at Pineda de Mar just as the town was beginning to stretch into life. The air was warm already, and the faint scent of coffee, and fresh bread was starting to linger in the breeze. We made the short eight-minute walk to the Hotel Altura Park, my home for the season, and as we turned the corner, I could already see the lobby beginning to buzz.

The early risers were on the move, hurrying down for breakfast before the queues began, and hotel staff were darting in all directions, uniforms neatly pressed, faces still fresh despite the growing heat. I pushed through the revolving doors, still slightly weary from the long night, and immediately caught a wave of smiles and recognition.

The receptionist looked up, beamed, and said, "Wesley, have you been out all night?"

"Yes," I replied with a tired grin. "Had to wait for a coach from the Czech Republic... ended up sleeping on a bench in Barcelona."

She burst out laughing, open-mouthed, belly laughing, and immediately turned to shout into the back office. Within seconds, a ripple of giggling and friendly mockery spread across the reception team and management to. A few waved, others gave me a mock round of applause. I just shook my head and laughed with them; it was that kind of hotel. Warm. Familiar. The sort of place where everyone knew your story before you'd even finished telling it.

I grabbed our room keys and took Lelena up to her room. She looked exhausted, understandably, and I asked if she fancied grabbing some breakfast. But she just shook her head and said she'd rather get some sleep first. Fair enough. I told her I was just a few doors down if she needed anything, and that I'd head down to the restaurant for a bite to eat.

Breakfast, after all, was sacred.

I wandered into the dining room, and there she was, Elisabeth, the German rep, sitting by the window with a cup of coffee and a small plate of pastries. She looked up, smiled, and waved me over.

"I thought your girlfriend was arriving last night?" she asked, scooting her plate to one side.

"She did," I said, collapsing into the chair across from her. "But the coach was delayed, didn't get in until after four and only just walked in the hotel thirty minutes ago. She's sleeping now. I'm starving. You know me, never one to miss breakfast."

Elisabeth smiled. "Yes, that's true. Always the early bird, you."

We chatted for a bit, catching up in the soft hum of the restaurant. I asked after her boyfriend, who I knew was due to visit soon. She shrugged slightly and gave a little sigh.

"Yes… next week. But honestly, I'm not sure I want him to come anymore. Things feel… different."

At the time, I simply nodded, sympathetic and understanding. I told her it would still be nice, maybe good for them. But looking back now, with the clarity of years and the wisdom of hindsight, I realise I completely missed the point. She wasn't just talking about her boyfriend. She was talking about me. That kind of quiet, hopeful nudge you don't catch until it's long gone.

We finished breakfast with the usual laughs and easy comfort we'd always had. As we stood to leave, she mentioned she wouldn't be covering Altura Park or the other nearby resorts for a few weeks, her boyfriend was visiting, then she'd be transferred to properties further up the coast, and someone else was covering in the meantime, but she would be back in several weeks' time.

At the time, I thought nothing of it. Just work shifts and holiday rotations. But now, decades later, I see it more clearly. She was creating space. Stepping back. Perhaps it was too difficult being around. Perhaps she'd hoped I'd see something I never did.

Experience teaches you these things, but only long after the moment's passed.

Still, we parted with a smile and the promise to catch up on her return, I gave her a hug, and which was longer than normal, and she seemed to cling on, I could feel her breath on my neck, and her breast against my chest, she kissed my cheek and then was gone. And for now, I had two weeks ahead with Lelena. And all the complicated, beautiful, and challenging emotions that would come with it.

The first few days with Lelena were, in many ways, refreshingly simple. There were no big dramas, no sudden changes of plan, just a steady blend of sun, sea, and a slightly chaotic schedule as I juggled being a good boyfriend and being a responsible overseas representative.

My working world hadn't slowed down just because she'd arrived. I was still zipping about the coast on the red devil moped, darting between seven properties, five hotels and two apartment blocks, checking on guests, smoothing over the odd issue, and running those little errands that came with keeping a region ticking along. It was high summer now, and the days blurred into each other in a kind of sun-soaked rhythm: check-ins, complaint handling, excursion bookings, and the constant battle with paperwork.

Meanwhile, Lelena was in her element. While I ran around in shirts damp with effort, and heavy red company blazer, she was gliding from poolside lounger to beach towel, bronzing gently in the Catalan sun, a paperback in hand and a cocktail never far from reach. At mealtimes, she'd pile her plate high with fruit, every colour under the sun, and by day three I'd started to wonder if she was in fact a fruit bat cleverly disguised as a Czech student. She loved it, the melons, the nectarines, the cherries, the citrus. She once returned from the buffet with a plate that looked more like a fruit stall in a local market. I teased her gently, of course. "You're going to turn into a mango," I said once, and she just smiled with that soft shrug of hers and took another bite of pineapple.

Despite the sweetness of those early days, I couldn't help but notice something was missing.

Not something dramatic, not even something I could fully explain at the time, but it was there, quietly. I realised I was missing Elisabeth. Not in a romantic sense, at least not consciously, but more in that every day, comforting way. I'd grown used to her being around. Our breakfasts and dinner together had become a kind of ritual. A dependable part of the chaos. The easy back-and-forth, the laughter, the quiet company that didn't require explaining.

Now, those breakfasts felt a little… empty. Not bad. Just different.

It was strange, having everything I thought I wanted in front of me, and still feeling a little off balance. Like someone had moved the furniture slightly when I wasn't looking. But I brushed it off. These were the early days. And summer had a long way yet to run.

A Day in the Clouds – Montserrat and the Bodega

We set off early, just after breakfast, still yawning from the long week but excited for a change of scenery. This time, it wasn't me doing the organising, well, not directly. I'd booked Lelena and myself onto one of the coach excursions that I'd arranged many times for guests, and now, for once, I was sitting in the passenger seat of experience.

It felt strange, boarding the coach as a customer rather than a rep. I was half-expecting someone to ask me to hand out rooming lists or run through the itinerary. Instead, I simply found a window seat, settled in next to Lelena, and for the first time in a while… just enjoyed the ride. The driver knew me, smiled and was a bit surprised I was not sitting at the front with the other guide to provide the tour.

The coach pulled away from the coast in that steady, low-gear rumble, leaving behind the heat of Pineda and the glint of the sea, and wound its way inland. As we climbed higher into the Catalan hills, the scenery began to change. The colours warmed, the landscape grew more rugged, and that soft, coastal breeze was replaced by the drier, more fragrant air of the Catalan countryside.

Out the window, we passed vineyards, sun-drenched olive groves, fields of dust, and clusters of terracotta-tiled villages that looked like they'd been untouched for a century. The roads became narrower and steeper, and every so often the coach would slow to a crawl on tight bends, with sheer drops just beyond the crash barriers. I glanced at Lelena, who didn't seem to mind, she was gazing out, camera in hand, sunglasses perched neatly, looking as content as I'd ever seen her.

Around us, the usual mix of curious tourists sat chatting softly, the occasional squeal of excitement when someone spotted a good photo opportunity or asked in hushed tones, "Is that Montserrat up ahead?" And then suddenly, there it was: Montserrat.

A strange and awe-inspiring sight, the serrated mountain ridge towering above the landscape like the fossilised spine of some ancient creature. The monastery buildings nestled impossibly into the cliffs, clinging to the rock as though they'd always been part of it. It didn't matter how many times you'd seen it; it always stopped you in your tracks.

The coach pulled into the designated parking area, and as we stepped off, I could already feel the change in the air — thinner, cooler, and carrying with it a kind of stillness I'd only ever felt in a few places. The kind that made you instinctively quieten your voice, as though the mountain itself was listening.

The real journey, up into the heart of the abbey, through the sacred corridors, past the Black Madonna, the panoramic viewpoints, the echoing halls of centuries-old prayers — that was still to come.

But the ride itself had already done something. It had drawn a line between the world we knew, the beach towels, the reps, the queues at reception, and this place, where time moved differently.

There's something about Montserrat that silences even the most talkative tourists. The moment you step off the coach and begin to ascend towards the monastery, it's as though the entire mountain puts it's finger to its lips. The air is laced with the scent of wild herbs and pine, a noticeable change from the salty tang of the coast. You don't need to be religious to feel it, that gentle pressure of reverence in the atmosphere. It's simply there.

We began our walk towards the Benedictine Abbey, joining the slow procession of visitors making their way up the winding paths and stepped walkways. Lelena walked just ahead, taking photos here and there, occasionally looking back with a smile that said, "This place is magic." And it was.

The architecture itself seemed to grow out of the rock, sandstone walls blending into the cliff face, ancient stairways carved with care, little arches and balconies perched impossibly high. It was both human and inhuman, shaped by hands but touched by something greater. The buildings stood not just as places of faith, but as testaments to patience, perseverance, and purpose.

We joined a guided group briefly, mostly to gain some context. The tour guide, a Catalan woman with a soft but assured voice, spoke in several languages and shared stories about the Black Madonna, the patron saint of Catalonia, housed inside the basilica. The line to see her up close was long, and Lelena and I decided to let the others shuffle through while we wandered further into the courtyard, taking in the views and sounds or rather, the lack of them.

Up there, the wind became a companion. It whispered around the corners of the buildings, rustled the dry grasses, and tugged gently at sleeves and hems. Everything felt amplified and yet still, like the mountain was breathing around you.

We stopped by one of the balconies that opened out to the most extraordinary view, a sweeping panorama of the Catalonian lowlands below, dotted with towns and vineyards and far-off mountain ridges in the distance. From that height, the world looked paused, like a painting or a dream.

"I feel so small," Lelena whispered beside me.

"That's the idea," I replied with a soft smile.

We sat for a while on a stone bench, just quietly taking it all in. No distractions, no rush. For once, I wasn't checking my watch or thinking about guests or timetables. Just the moment, two people on a ledge, half a mile above the noise of life.

We visited the small gift shop, naturally, where Lelena bought a small gift, and I picked up a postcard I'd never send. It's probably still in a drawer somewhere. We shared a coffee at the little terrace café, watching new visitors arrive as the earlier ones filed back towards their coaches. Everyone had the same look, a kind of softened, awed quietness, like their shoulders had dropped just a little lower after arriving.

As the midday sun began to climb and the bells rang out in low, steady rhythm, our guide called us back to the coach. The visit had only been a few hours long, but it felt like we'd stepped outside time for a while, a quiet breath in the middle of the chaotic Spanish summer.

We climbed back onto the coach, sun-kissed and smiling, and as the engine fired up and we began the slow descent down the mountain roads, I felt something shift, not just in me, but between us.

A deeper calm. A new stillness.

And we still had the bodega to come.

The Bodega Challenge...

If Montserrat had been the soul of the day, then the bodega was undoubtedly the spirit, in every sense of the word.

After descending from the mountains, our coach rolled gently through the sun-drenched countryside towards one of the region's most well-known wine bodegas. Nestled between fields of vines and shaded by a scattering of olive trees, it was a long, low building, with thick whitewashed walls, arched doorways, and the slightly mischievous air of a place that had seen many an overambitious visitor leave with a wobble in their step.

Now, I'd done this trip before, or at least, something very similar, back in the 1980s with my mum and dad. I remember it well. My father had made a gallant effort of getting around as many barrels as he could, and I swear he got dangerously close to the full tour. I think the final count was somewhere around the high thirties, though by that stage no one could be sure if he was still going or just doubling back for seconds.

We ended up with seventeen bottles of wine. Getting them home to the UK was no easy feat, this was well before the days of relaxed customs allowances. We had bottles stashed in socks, stuffed in clothes, and wrapped in beach towels all within the suitcase. I wouldn't be surprised if one or two were still hidden in a loft somewhere in Kent.

So naturally, when the guide at the bodega stood up and, with a grin, announced to the group, "There are two hundred and ninety-seven barrels here… and no one has ever completed the lot," I couldn't help but smirk.

The challenge was issued with a wink, part joke, part dare. Everyone laughed. Glasses were handed out, the size of large thimbles, and the rules were simple: try as many as you like, go at your own pace, and don't forget to write down the ones you like, just in case you remember them tomorrow.

The room itself was spectacular, long vaulted ceilings, old wooden beams, cool stone floors, and then, stretching out in every direction, rows upon rows of oak wine barrels, each with a tap, a tiny chalkboard label, and a soft invitation to sip.

Lelena and I took our time, drifting between barrels, comparing notes, sharing surprised looks when one was particularly strong or suspiciously fruity. There were reds as bold as bullfighters, whites as light as Catalan breeze, and sweet muscats that tasted more like dessert than wine.

The atmosphere among the group turned into a low, merry hum, voices rising, cheeks pinking, a few overconfident souls declaring they were "making a serious go at the record." One poor chap, after about fifteen, sat down on a bench and declared, "I've gone blind in one eye," though it turned out to just be a smudge on his sunglasses.

I must have tried ten or twelve before I realised, I was already slightly to cheerful to count accurately. Lelena, who was much more sensible, had stopped after four and turned to fruit and olives from the nearby tasting table. "I'll drive," she joked, even though we were on a coach.

At the end of the visit, the inevitable purchases began. People filled baskets with bottles, most insisting they were "for gifts" though we all knew they wouldn't make it past the hotel room. I picked up a couple myself, one that reminded me of the bodega I'd visited with my mum and dad, and one sweet red that Lelena had liked. Something to remember the day by.

We boarded the coach with a soft buzz of satisfaction, the sun now starting to lower in the sky. Laughter trickled down the aisles, bags of wine clinked under the seats, and somewhere behind us, someone was already snoring gently.

As we pulled away, I looked out across the vines, all golden and green in the afternoon light, and thought how funny it is, the way life circles back. The barrels, the laughter, the people you love beside you.

Once with my parents. Now with her.

And even if I'd never make it to all 297… I reckon I gave it a good go.

Back to Pineda – and the Last Few Days …

The journey back from Montserrat and the Bodega was a quiet one. Not because anything was wrong, quite the opposite. It was the sort of comfortable silence that comes after a full day, when you've said most of what needs saying and are just enjoying the warm buzz of the road home. The coach hummed, the sun dipped, and we drifted past vineyards and sleepy Catalan villages like they'd been painted on glass.

Back in Pineda, the days blurred gently, beach mornings, shared meals, the occasional dash on my red moped to check in on guests or cover a transfer. Lelena fell into the rhythm easily, lounging by the pool or and enjoying the hotel meals.

It was lovely, in that quiet sort of way. Simple. Familiar. But of course, it couldn't last forever.

Saying Goodbye …

Of course, I did the very British thing.

I helped with her bags, smiled far too much, said something awkwardly upbeat like, "Safe journey and don't forget your fruit stash!" and waved like I was on a royal balcony. Lelena smiled through the coach window, that quiet sort of smile you give when words have all been used up, tears in her eyes.

Then she was gone.

I stood for a moment longer than I needed to, like some tragic figure from a slow-motion movie scene, before realising the coach had long disappeared and I was now just a bloke loitering outside a hotel holding an empty bottle of water.

Naturally, I walked back in, nodded at reception as if I'd just popped out for a drink, and returned to normal activities.

No time for moping, reps don't get emotional days off. The welcome meetings still needed running, the complaints were still coming in, and Sergi would likely be shouting at me to go surfing as I had not seen them much in two weeks.

And besides, I had a reputation to uphold.

Casanova of the Costa, remember?

Well... at least until the next chapter.

Chapter Nine

You need to understand that the life of a rep overseas is very intense. It's not all partying, snorting the local cocktail up your nose, or some kind of rolling orgy with guests. It involves a lot of really hard work.

You've got rooming lists to go over for every arrival, and they must match up perfectly with the bookings. You make sure all the special requests are sorted, sea view rooms, twin beds instead of doubles, adjoining balconies for couples who can't bear to be apart (or, ironically, couples trying to keep their distance).

And I'm not just talking about a quick glance at a list; I'm talking about physically walking the rooms. In my case, I'd visit every single property I managed, and if the guests hadn't arrived yet, I'd check the rooms myself. Toilets flushing properly? Tick. Taps running hot? Tick. Balcony chairs not held together with string. Tick. Towels present? Hopefully. Cockroaches? Only the ones paying for half-board. (I'm joking… or am I?)

Now, yes, there were some companies where the reps went completely off the rails. You probably remember them. Club 18–30, for example, the ones who welcomed guests with goodie bags containing more condoms than conversation. And fair play to them, that was their market.

But that wasn't me.

I took a different approach. More senior, more professional. Not because I was trying to be better than anyone else, but because I genuinely cared about the guests, the brand I worked for, and my job. I saw myself as a kind of frontline ambassador.

And don't forget, when disaster struck (and it often did), it was us reps who were the first on the scene.

So, when I say that what happened with Sofía caught me off guard, you'll understand why.

Because for all my years of handling awkward arrivals, lost luggage, broken air conditioning, and guests with attitudes bigger than their passports, nothing quite prepared me for Sofía.

The Hotel Altura Park was part of a well-known chain that dotted the Catalan coastline, a string of properties on both sides of Barcelona, each humming along with its own rhythm, yet all connected by a central headquarters in the city of Tarragona. Every so often, a member of the group's head office staff would come up to Pineda de Mar to check in on the finances, smooth over any operational creases, and remind everyone that corporate still had its eye on things.

At first, these visits were fairly uneventful. A young Spanish chap arrived, all smiles and spreadsheets, who spent his time bouncing between the manager's office and the hotel café, never once disturbing the flow of life in the lobby.

But by summer, the rhythm shifted.

Because in walked Señorita Sofía.

She wasn't like the others. She swept in with the confidence of someone born for corner offices and candlelit balconies. She wore her hair tied back in a tight, elegant ponytail, her makeup was minimal but flawless, and her suit, a rich cream ensemble with navy piping, looked like it had been designed by someone with a love of timeless Spanish tailoring and a bank account to match. She had the sort of presence that made receptionists sit up straighter and made you second guess whether your shirt needed ironing again.

It was mid-afternoon when I first saw her properly. I'd walked up to the reception desk to double-check the latest rooming list, another batch of guests were due that evening, and I wanted to be sure their requests had been handled. Lucía, my favourite receptionist, was on duty.

Now Lucía was a story all on her own. Young, gentle, and effortlessly beautiful in that quiet Catalan way, she had the kind of eyes that made you want to tell her secrets and a smile that softened even the most irate German guest. She was engaged to a man in St Albans and regularly told me with excitement about her plans to move to England in 1993. What this fiancé had done to deserve her, I'll never know. But I always enjoyed our chats, especially when we shared evening walks as she made her way home and I strolled toward the square to catch the Sardana dancing. There was nothing romantic in it, not really. Just two people enjoying the comfort of each other's company under a Spanish sky.

But that afternoon, Lucía wasn't alone.

"Wesley," she said, lighting up as I approached. "You must meet Señorita Sofía, from Tarragona."

Sofía stood, gracefully, and offered her hand. It was warm, firm, and lingered a second longer than it needed to. Her voice had that soft, velvet Spanish tone, and when she said, "Encantada," I could've sworn I saw the faintest blush dust her cheeks.

Later that evening, after dealing with another whirlwind of check-ins and a minor complaint about a plug socket that mysteriously "exploded" (it didn't), I found myself meandering into the hotel bar. Just a quiet drink, I thought. Nothing fancy.

A wind-down moment with a bit of live music before turning in.

And there she was.

Señorita Sofía. Alone at a table near the corner, a glass of red wine in front of her, tapping a manicured nail to the rhythm of the guitarist playing soft flamenco in the corner.

Now, I'm not one to hover, but I'd been raised properly. So, I walked over, polite, casual, and before I could even greet her, she looked up with a smile that could have launched ten ships.

"Hola, Señor Wesley," she said warmly, her eyes bright.

"¿Qué tal?" I asked, easing into my best rep-Castilian.

"Muy bueno," she replied, then gestured gracefully to the empty chair opposite her.

Well... what's a man to do?

Her hand was cool to the touch, her smile even warmer. I sat, a little more aware of my shirt collar than I had been all day, and ordered a drink, something simple, something slow, a nice brandy with water seems perfect. The bar wasn't busy, just a handful of tourists finishing off their sangria pitchers and the guitarist in the corner coaxing melancholy from nylon strings.

"So," she began, her voice low and smooth, "you are the famous Señor Wesley I've heard about in Tarragona?"

I laughed, unsure if she was joking or if my reputation had somehow made its way down the coast. "Only if they're saying good things," I replied.

She leaned in slightly. "Oh... they say you're very professional. Very... efficient."

Now, look, I've had compliments before. But this one, in that tone, over candlelight, with her eyes catching mine just long enough to hold them, felt... different.

We spoke for over an hour. About work. About life. She told me about her fiancé, a quiet man from a small town near Tarragona who worked in logistics. Her eyes didn't light up when she said his name. She didn't speak ill of him, not at all, but the warmth that had been in her voice moments before dimmed ever so slightly.

I returned the honesty, told her about Lelena, my Czech girlfriend, and how we'd known each other for years and she had gone home after visiting me. And yet, even as I said the words, they felt distant. A script I knew by heart, but one that didn't quite fit the moment I was living.

Sofía swirled her wine slowly in the glass. "Love is complicated, no?" she said, not really asking.

"Sometimes it's not," I said. "Sometimes we just make it that way."

That earned a smile. A real one. And for a few seconds, the silence between us said far more than any words.

But I was still a professional. I'd always drawn the line when it needed drawing, and this was one of those moments.

I checked my watch. It was nearly midnight.

"I should go," I said, rising slowly. "Another busy day tomorrow, and I promised myself I'd get some actual sleep."

Sofía stood as well, smoothing her clothes with one graceful motion. "You're very disciplined," she teased.

"I have to be. Chaos always finds me eventually," I grinned.

She looked at me, her eyes soft. "Would you… have breakfast with me tomorrow? Just something simple. In the restaurant, around eight?"

I hesitated, not because I didn't want to, but because I knew what it could mean. Still, I nodded.

"I'd like that."

And then, as the candle flickered between us, I reached for her hand. Not to shake it, not even really to hold it, just to bring it gently to my lips. One kiss, light and proper, the kind they used to write about in books before everything became a swipe left or right.

"Buenas noches, Señorita Sofía."

"Buenas noches, Wesley," she said quietly.

She turned and walked away toward the other wing of the hotel, heels clicking on the polished floor, the scent of her perfume lingering long after she disappeared around the corner.

I stood there for a moment longer than I should have, watching the empty corridor where she'd been, before heading upstairs to bed, alone.

Sleep didn't come easy that night…

The Morning After…

Eight o'clock was late for me.

By then, most days, I'd already be in full swing, zipping between properties, answering phone calls, or chasing down towels for guests who thought they were on holiday with the Royal Family. But that morning, I'd made time. Made space.

And before the sun had properly risen, I slipped out of the Altura Park through the beach entrance and wandered down towards the shoreline.

The Mediterranean was still waking up. At six in the morning, the light had that soft, honeyed hue that makes you pause, even when you've seen it a hundred times. The sea was calm, whispering rather than speaking, it's surface smooth and silver in the early sun. I kicked off my shoes and walked barefoot across the cool, fine pebble-sand of Pineda's beach. A few local fishermen were already out, casting silently from the beach, there silhouettes barely moving against the swell.

Without thinking much of it, I peeled off my shirt and walked straight into the water. It wasn't cold, just refreshing, the kind of temperature that shakes off the cobwebs and makes you feel alive again. I swam for a while. Just me, the sea, and the slowly climbing sun. For a moment, everything was quiet. Still. Centred.

Back at the hotel, I showered, changed into my uniform, white shirt, pressed trousers, name badge just so — and glanced at the time. 7:58 AM.

Perfect.

The restaurant at Altura Park was bright and airy, with tall windows that welcomed the morning light like an old friend. The breakfast area faced out towards the pool and beyond to the sea, a view so picturesque that guests would often take twice as long over there toast just to soak it in. There was the familiar scent of coffee and toasted bread, the soft clinking of cutlery, the murmur of multiple languages being spoken in lazy morning tones.

She was already there, seated at a table just by the window, a fresh-squeezed orange juice in front of her, and, of course, that knowing smile. Sofía.

I walked over and greeted her as naturally as I could, though the truth is, I felt just a little out of place, not because I wasn't meant to be there, but because I wasn't entirely sure what this was.

She looked radiant. Crisp white linen blouse, hair down this time, and a simple silver pendant resting gently at her collarbone. The kind of look that said effortless elegance without needing to try.

"Buenos días, Wesley," she said softly.

"Buenos días, Señorita Sofía," I replied with a nod, slipping into the seat opposite her. "You've already beaten me here."

"I've been looking forward to this," she said, with that same calm confidence she'd worn the night before.

We chatted lightly about the weather, the finance tasks, the quirks of running hotel operations with so many hotels. She asked me about my morning, and I told her truthfully about the swim, the light, the fishermen.

"You're becoming more Spanish, or I should say Catalan every day," she teased.

"Well," I said, smiling, "I did consider showing up late and blaming it on a siesta."

She laughed, and there was something about that laugh. Unforced. Warm. Like a secret shared.

But time, as always, was ticking.

I was due in Calella by 9:30 AM for a welcome meeting, covering multiple hotels in one go, a proper rollout of the local excursions, essentials, and dos and don'ts. Over 50 guests had arrived the day before, so I needed to be sharp. Then it would be straight back to Altura Park for another smaller session at 11:00 AM. Fortunately, those guests were already lounging by the pool with drinks in hand, and I'd agreed to do the welcome meeting right there, relaxed, informal. The perfect balance.

"I have to head off shortly," I said, finishing the last of my coffee. "Calella's calling."

Sofía nodded. "Duty calls."

"Always does."

We stood together. There was a pause, not awkward, but full. Like we both knew we were at the edge of something but neither of us was quite ready to step over it.

"I must tell you," She said softly, brushing an invisible thread from her blouse, "I'm returning to Tarragona later this morning. But I'll be back early next week... and I do hope we can meet again." She let the words hang for a moment before adding with a playful smile, "I might just miss you a little."

Her tone wasn't overly forward, but it didn't need to be. The message was there, tucked neatly beneath the smile and the careful choice of words.

I returned the smile. "I'll look forward to it."

We held the moment just a beat longer, and then in the same manner as the night before, I kissed her hand gently.

"Safe journey, Señorita."

"Gracias, Wesley, Casanova" she said, her voice dipping slightly as she grinned.

She watched me go.

And as I stepped out into the already warming day, I couldn't help but feel that something had shifted ever so slightly. Not just the temperature, but something in the air between us. Something that, by next week, might need answering.

Calella Calling

The engine of the red devil, my trusty old moped, coughed into life with its usual drama and gusto. I strapped my bag tight, tugged on my sunglasses, and zipped out from the rear of Altura Park, past the old bull ring, which was now a citrus orchard, heading south along the sea front towards Calella.

There was a certain joy in those early morning rides. The sun still casting long shadows, the salty breeze in my face, and the distant shimmer of the sea beside me. I weaved through the narrow backstreets with ease, dodging delivery vans, sleepy-eyed locals setting up shop, and the occasional cyclist trying to beat the heat.

As I dropped down to the beachfront road, I couldn't resist a cheeky detour, a short dash along the firm sand where the beach met the concrete path, tyres humming across the grains. The coast was waking up: umbrellas going up, café chairs scraping into place, lifeguards stretching on the beach, getting ready for another long day of heat and hollering.

And then, just ahead, a cluster of familiar faces, guests from the transfer the night before, already dressed for the beach and waving excitedly as I approached.

I gave a theatrical hoot of the horn and raised a hand in salute.

"Oi oi, Wesley!" someone shouted. I responded with "I will have a sangria waiting for you when you arrive!"

The group erupted in cheers and laughter as I grinned and shouted back, before zooming off again, the red devil roaring back up onto the main road like a knight charging into battle, minus the horse, plus a rattling two-stroke engine.

The hotel I was headed for sat at the back of Calella, a large, concrete number with big package holiday energy and an army of sunburnt lobster-coloured bodies lounging outside already. As I pulled in and parked the moped, I took a deep breath.

Welcome meetings

Now, they sound simple enough, you stand up, you smile, you tell people where the pool is and try to sell them a few trips. But in Costa Brava, they were a bloody minefield. This region, bless it, had been through two solid decades of mass tourism. Everyone and their auntie had already done the excursions. Montserrat? Been there. Medieval knight show? Yawn. Barcelona city tour? Again?

To make it trickier, this time of year brought in the budget wave, those bargain holidaymakers who'd snagged a £145 deal for ten nights, full or half board, and turned up with barely enough cash for bottled water, let alone a day trip to Girona.

Still, we reps were trained to try, and I always did my best, I needed the commission because we were paid poorly in general, and the commission was crucial at times. I stood there in my crisp shirt, talking up the Olympic village tour, giving it all the passion I could muster. I pushed the Medieval Knight

Tournament like it was the West End's next big hit, sold the Montserrat pilgrimage like a spiritual awakening, and tried, desperately to breathe some cultural excitement into Girona, which in truth was my personal favourite.

But Girona... oh, Girona. Full of charm, history, colour, and absolutely no takers. It was like trying to sell Shakespeare to a stag do in Benidorm. It is just not happening!

Still, I gave it everything. Smiles, stories, inside tips, and the odd joke at my own expense. Because even when they didn't buy the excursions, if they laughed, if they felt welcomed, if they remembered my name, then I'd done the job.

And truthfully? I loved it. The performance, the pressure, the oddball characters in every group.

Just another morning in paradise.

I'd barely finished my pitch for the Medieval Knight Tournament (complete with exaggerated sword movements and a noble "Huzzah!") when a woman in the third row raised her hand, not to ask a question, but to produce a thermos flask.

"Wesley, love," she called out, in a thick Birmingham accent, "Do you reckon I can fill this up with sangria and take it on the beach?"

I blinked. "Technically... no. But morally? Absolutely."

She grinned and gave me a wink, stowing the thermos away like a secret weapon.

Then came a man, Scottish, deeply tanned, and dressed like Indiana Jones, who leaned forward with a very serious question.

"This tour to Barcelona... will we be back in time for BBC World Service on the TV?"

I paused, unsure whether this was a joke. It wasn't.

"Well," I replied, "you might miss the news, but you'll have seen the Sagrada Familia, which is probably more impressive than the news at home"

He nodded solemnly. "Thanks, ok, sounds good"

And of course, no welcome meeting would be complete without that one guest, the professional complainer, who hadn't even unpacked but was already preparing a legal case against the room's curtains for being "to blue."

"Wesley," she said, frowning at her notepad (yes, notepad), "why is the swimming pool in sunlight all afternoons?"

"Well, madam," I said with a perfectly straight face, "we've arranged for the sun to cross the sky in just that way to enhance your tan."

She did not laugh. But the couple next to her did. Loudly.

After the formalities were wrapped up, a few guests hung around, some genuinely interested in trips, others just wanting a chat. A little girl shyly handed me a drawing of "Wesley the Rep" complete with sunglasses, moped, and a cape.

"Apparently I'm a superhero now," I told her parents.

"You must be," the dad replied, "dealing with this lot of plonkers."

We all laughed, and I felt that familiar rush, the joy of connection. Of being that friendly face of Britain in a foreign land, making people feel safe, entertained, and understood. Even if they did ask you to change the position of the sun, they really relied on the British way, that of a person who controls things and tells them where the line is so they can form up nicely.

Back at Altura Park

By the time I pulled back into the rear of Hotel Altura Park, the midday sun was already blazing, and the tiles on the entrance steps were hot enough to fry an egg. I parked up the red devil, straightened my shirt, and strolled through the cool reception lobby like a man with a plan, because, well, I did. I glanced over for Sofía, but she had gone, so onward I went.

It was time for my second welcome meeting of the day. This one, however, was different. Just a couple of arrivals last night in this hotel, hardly worth dragging out the full flipchart and spiel. But I had another idea. I was going to do it my way.

I popped into the bar, where Manuel, the hotel's head barman, a brilliant man with a moustache that deserved its own passport, was polishing glasses with military precision.

"Manuel," I said, with the conspiratorial tone of a man about to bend the rules slightly, "I need a favour."

His eyebrow raised. "How many?"

"Six bottles of champagne, four jugs of sangria, three jugs of orange juice, and plenty of glasses — with ice. Deliver them to the poolside terrace, under the big umbrella by the shallow end. I'll sign for it all. Cosmos Holidays. Muchas gracias, jefe."

He grinned and gave a small salute. "You throw better fiestas than management."

Moments later, as I set up a couple of tables and pulled the umbrella across to provide some shade, the drinks began arriving like a royal banquet. The fizz, the fruit, the colours, it looked like a wedding reception was about to start.

Now, you might say that's a bit much for a welcome meeting with just two guests. But here's the thing: I didn't see it that way.

Around the pool lounged the rest of my guests, familiar faces from earlier weeks, regulars on their third trip of the year, couples who'd remembered my name and asked after me the day before. Interspersed among them were hundreds of sun-seared Thomson Holidays customers, sipping their lukewarm house drinks and eyeing my setup with curiosity.

I walked over to the first few sunbeds and raised a hand.

"Hi everyone, I've got a welcome meeting here for a couple of new arrivals, but I've got plenty of drinks for all my Cosmos guests. Champagne, sangria, orange juice, whatever you fancy. Come and join me by the umbrella, have a drink on us, and let's make it a proper catch-up."

They were up in seconds, like meerkats after a whistle. Glasses clinked, laughter sparked, and the buzz was immediate. One of my guests, already halfway into her flute of fizz, turned to a nearby Thomson group and declared with a grin:

"I bet you don't get this with Thomson!"

I pretended not to hear it, but inside, I was beaming.

I knew, without a doubt, that by that evening, the Thomson reps would be getting asked all sorts of awkward questions. And that by tomorrow, I'd have earned myself a cheeky little reputation.

But that's what set me apart. I didn't just do the job, I lived it. And when you're living it, you bring others along for the ride.

Even if that ride includes slightly more champagne than the training manual suggests.

Later That Evening...

By the time the heat of the day melted into the mellow warmth of evening, Altura Park was in full swing. Guests were fresh from the pool, sun-kissed and buzzing from the afternoon fizz. Some were prepping for dinner, others lingering in the lobby or strolling lazily along the promenade. I'd slipped into something more relaxed, smart shirt, sleeves rolled, a splash of kouros cologne, I look dialled to "evening casual."

I made my way to the bar to grab a drink before heading out for dinner with some returning guests. As I approached, I spotted Manuel behind the bar, gleaming glasses stacked high like trophies of a successful day's campaign.

He caught my eye instantly.

"Señor Wesley," he said in that deep, theatrical voice of his, polishing a wine glass with excessive flair. "Today you were el campeón — the poolside king."

I laughed. "Just keeping the guests happy, Manuel. You know the drill."

He leaned in a little closer, lowering his voice to a conspiratorial tone.

"And Sofía..." he said, drawing the name out like a love song, "you looked good together. A fine match. If you succeed — muy afortunado, amigo."

I gave him a half smile, shook my head. "Purely platonic, my friend."

Manuel raised a single eyebrow in a manner worthy of Roger Moore, and I swear, I swear his moustache curled upward at the ends like a pair of Spanish quotation marks. He didn't say another word, just gave a small bow and poured me a brandy on ice, sliding it across the bar with the flair of a magician.

I turned to head off, and that's when the Thomson reps arrived.

Two of them, freshly suited and visibly flustered, marched in like detectives on a case.

"Wesley," one of them said, arms folded. "Poolside champagne at a welcome meeting?"

I sipped my drink. "Was there a noise complaint?"

"No, but…" He hesitated. "We've had at least a dozen guests ask us why we don't do 'the Wesley treatment'."

I nodded thoughtfully. "That's a fair question."

The other rep, a younger lad with far too much gel in his hair, piped up. "You'll ruin the budget for the rest of us."

"Only if you let me," I replied with a grin.

There was a pause. The older rep narrowed his eyes. "You're trouble, you know that?"

"Only the good kind," I said, raising my glass and walking off to the sound of Manuel chuckling behind me and muttering something that sounded like, "Casanova strikes again…"

And just like that, another legend was born, not just for the guests, but firmly whispered among the reps to.

Several Nights Later: Fire and Finesse

It was just past 11:30 PM and I'd just returned from an unusually civilised dinner with a couple of regular guests, older pair from Yorkshire who loved to regale me with tales of Torremolinos in the '70s and insisted I try their homemade marmalade from back home. I'd barely kicked off my shoes when the phone in my room rang.

Reception.

"Señor Wesley, es urgente — the hotel in Calella... está en fuego!"

I was on my feet in a heartbeat, still buttoning my shirt as I bounded out of the door, grabbed my keys, and launched myself onto the red devil, my moped. I didn't even have time to curse the dodgy battery-powered headlight, but I did remember to frantically pedal just enough to keep it from going dim. It was like engaging "turbo mode," Flintstones style. Pedal, buzz, roar, and I was off.

Barrelling through the darkened streets, wind in my hair and heart pounding, I zigzagged through the sleepy lanes of Calella like a man possessed. Tourists were stumbling out of late-night bars, drunk on sangria or beer and unaware of the drama unfolding just up the hill.

And then I saw it, smoke billowing out the side windows of the Hotel, a budget 2-star tucked behind the resort centre like an afterthought. The flicker of emergency lights, the sharp scent of burning wood and plastic, the distant crackle of a radio over the sound of the fire crew shouting instructions. It wasn't towering flames, but it was serious, thick, choking smoke filled the upper floors.

I had 76 guests in that building. Every one of them on the kind of ultra-discounted holiday that had their package price lower than the average taxi fare from the airport to the resort. £125 to £175 for 7 or 14 nights, half board or full board — depending on which poor soul had clicked the "upgrade" checkbox.

I burst through the crowd of onlookers and started shouting names, getting a headcount, moving everyone across the street into a safer, clearer area.

"All Cosmos guests, please come to me now. Stick together. Stay calm. I need a full roll call, and I need it now."

Hands were raised. Names called. One older lady asked if she could go back for her tea bags. I gave her a firm "no" and kept the list moving.

Once I'd confirmed everyone was safe and out, I turned to the group.

"I need 20 minutes. Please stay right here, don't move — and try not to breathe to deeply." I managed a faint smile, though my heart was racing.

Then I bolted.

I flew down the slope to one of the finest hotels in Calella. A 4-star gem I'd eaten in occasionally and only ever had a few guests in. It was the kind of place where the tablecloths were thick, the staff wore gloves, and the coffee came with a little square of chocolate on the side.

I skidded into the lobby like something from an 80s action film, startling the receptionist.

"I need to speak to the manager — now. It's urgent."

The manager appeared from the office, half-asleep but still wearing his tie.

"Fire at one of my hotels," I said, breathlessly. "I have 76 guests — I need rooms. They've been evacuated. Can you help?"

To his credit, he didn't flinch. He took a beat, tapped into his ledger, and said, "We have availability… about 90 beds. If you need them, they are yours."

"Done," I said. "I will bring them here within the hour, they have no clothing other than what they are wearing."

Back I went, smoke still lingering in the air as the fire crew continued dampening down.

I explained the situation calmly, professionally, as if this sort of thing happened every week.

"Ladies and gents, here's what's happening. You're going to be re-housed, complimentary, at one of the top hotels in town. Closer to the beach. Bigger rooms. No cost to you. Your meals will continue as per your original booking. Just please, stay calm, and follow me."

The guests looked at one another, murmured their approval, and gathered there few things. Even the tea bag lady gave me a wink.

We walked down the hill together, 76 weary, smoke-scented tourists and one sharply dressed rep on a mission, into the warm Catalan night, toward comfort, safety, and a damned good breakfast in the morning.

Return of the Catalan Princess

A few days had passed since the fire, and life, as it always does in Spain, had slowly returned to its rhythmic hum. Transfers, excursions, hotel inspections, rooming list corrections, awkward lost-luggage conversations, and one particularly bizarre episode involving a guest who swore their television remote controlled the ceiling fan, business as usual.

It was hot. The kind of heat that clings to you like a second skin. The Costa Brava was in full summer bloom, with holidaymakers roasting like rotisserie chickens on plastic loungers, and the air filled with the scent of suntan lotion, grilled sardines, and the occasional whiff of cheap aftershave.

I'd just finished checking a coachload into the Altura Park and was about to head to the desk area to update the excursion board when something, someone, caught the corner of my eye.

Sofía.

She'd entered the lobby like a whisper on the wind, yet somehow everything paused for a second. Conversations seemed to dip, the clatter of suitcase wheels fell away, and for the briefest of moments, my heart stopped.

There she was, looking utterly radiant, classic, composed, and impossibly elegant despite the 35°C heat. While most of us were half-melted and mildly deranged from the sun, Sofía looked like she had just stepped off the set of a Mediterranean perfume commercial.

She saw me. A slow, knowing smile curled across her lips and she gave a small wave, walking smoothly to the reception desk with the grace of someone who knew exactly how much attention she was drawing, and quite possibly enjoyed it.

I nodded in return, politely, then, to avoid looking like some lovesick schoolboy or eager stalker, I casually slipped away.

Room. Siesta. Hide.

To be fair, it had been an incredibly demanding week. The hotel fire had taken it's toll, emotionally and physically. My eyes were aching, my legs felt like bricks, and I was due to meet Sergi and the surf crew later that evening for a low-key celebration, one of the surf girls had a birthday, and there was already talk of schnapps and poorly sung Catalan songs.

I told myself I needed the rest. And I did. But the truth?

I needed space. A moment. Because Sofía's return had tilted the axis again, and I wasn't sure if I was quite ready to lean into it.

But something told me... I'd have to soon.

The evening with the surf crew started just as I expected, loud, rowdy, warm-hearted, and fuelled by a steady stream of schnapps and mischief. We gathered at a small beachfront chiringuito in Santa Susanna, a scrappy but beloved local spot with bamboo chairs that wobbled and music that never quite made it to the chorus without skipping.

Sergi was in fine form, Bruno was telling a story none of us could quite follow, and a round of peach schnapps appeared out of nowhere, courtesy of someone's cousin's birthday. The night buzzed with laughter and that summer-night kind of madness that only ever happens when you're young, half-sunburnt, and completely surrounded by people who feel like family.

But somewhere around the third schnapps, I found myself zoning out, not rudely, but gently. Like I'd left the party without leaving the table. I suddenly knew I didn't want to stay late, didn't want to shout over the music, didn't want to pretend I was entirely present when, clearly, I wasn't.

By 8 PM, I made my excuses "early transfer tomorrow," "need to write up the room reports," "you lot are too wild for me" and gave them my trademark hang loose salute and lopsided grin before hopping on my moped.

I rode the coastline slowly, letting the cool breeze undo some of the day's heat, and parked up at the Altura Park. Instead of heading straight inside, I wandered down to the quieter poolside bar, that peaceful little spot where guests sat watching the light fade across the sea, with wine in hand and conversation just a soft murmur against the breeze.

And there she was.

Sofía.

Sitting alone, legs crossed, a glass of white wine catching the last golden rays like a prism. She looked utterly at ease, her jacket draped over the back of her chair, her hair pinned up in that effortless way that only ever seems to work in European women.

She turned her head, noticed me, and smiled, not the kind of smile you throw to strangers, but something softer. Familiar. She lifted her hand in a small, beckoning wave and said with a quiet sincerity, "Wesley… come. Sit with me."

I walked over, my nerves strangely alive, and eased into the chair beside her. "Hola," I offered, keeping it light.

"I asked after you," she said, her eyes fixed on mine now. "They told me about the fire. About what you did for those guests. I... I came back a day early. To see that you were okay."

I blinked, surprised. "That's kind of you."

She shrugged, then smiled again, that knowing smile that said she didn't do it just to be kind.

"Also," she added, "I thought I might enjoy a quiet drink... and good company."

I leaned back in the chair, nodded slowly, and signalled the waiter for two more glasses of whatever she was drinking. The waves gentle rolled in quietly onto the small pebbles of the beach. The candles on the bar tables flickered in the dusk. And I suddenly realised that maybe, just maybe, this evening was about to unfold into something quite different from the one I'd originally planned some days ago.

The wine kept coming, though I stopped noticing how many glasses we'd had. We talked and we laughed, really laughed, the kind that leaves your cheeks aching and your soul lighter. Somewhere between politics and paella, between travel tales and tales we probably shouldn't have told, I found myself utterly lost in her company.

She wasn't just beautiful, though she absolutely was, she was sharp, funny, full of mischief, and not afraid to tease. But there was something else. A softness beneath the sharpness. A kind of unspoken sadness maybe, or perhaps just the weight of responsibility that comes with being someone who's always "got it together."

And I suppose, in that moment, we were both tired of being the ones who always had it together.

The hours passed, unnoticed. By the time I glanced at my watch, the hands had crept towards midnight. The hotel bar was beginning it's gentle wind-down, the soft clink of bottles being shelved, the barman's subtle glances at the clock, the slow stacking of empty chairs.

Still, we didn't move.

Eventually, she looked at me and smiled with a trace of reluctance. "They'll be putting the lights off next."

"Reckon they might turn the hose on us if we don't move," I replied, laughing, standing up and offering my hand to her like it was the most natural thing in the world.

She took it without hesitation.

We walked slowly through the quiet hotel lobby, still my hand gently touching her hand. I became hyper-aware of how soft hers felt in mine, how strange, and yet familiar, this felt. There was no awkwardness. Just a quiet comfort, like we'd done this a hundred times before.

"I'll walk you to your room," I said gently, not asking, just stating.

"Of course," she replied, her voice suddenly smaller, almost shy.

We took the stairs, climbing slowly. Our footsteps echoed faintly on the marble tiles, and every now and again we'd glance sideways at each other, small smiles forming and fading.

We reached her floor.

The corridor was dimly lit, the old-fashioned wall sconces casting a golden glow that felt like it belonged in a painting. We stopped outside her room. For a moment, we just stood there.

Sofía turned, key in hand, and opened the door. Then, without a word, she stepped close. So, close I could feel the warmth of her skin, smell the faint perfume she wore — subtle, floral, not overpowering.

She leaned in.

And kissed me.

It was gentle. Soft. Not rushed or dramatic like something in a film. Just… right. Natural. Like we'd arrived at this point not through a script, but through real life. A thousand tiny moments leading to this one.

For a moment, I froze, more out of surprise than hesitation. And then I didn't. My hand moved to her back. Her fingertips brushed my arm.

When we pulled apart, we didn't speak.

She turned toward me at the threshold, her eyes shimmering under the dim light of the corridor. There was no hesitation now, just a quiet storm between us, waiting to be acknowledged.

"I came back early… because of you," she said, her voice low but steady. "And now I don't want this night to end."

She smiled again, not the same playful grin from earlier, but something softer, warmer, more uncertain. Then, without a word, she stepped through the door and gently pulled me in with her.

There was no door closing between us.

There was only the moment, wide open, and the impossible pull of two lives briefly, maybe dangerously, colliding.

I reached out, took her hand, and crossed the threshold.

The room was quiet, dimly lit by the hallway light still spilling in through the open door. She closed it gently behind us and flicked on a lamp, not the harsh overhead light, but a low one near the bed, casting everything in a golden, calming glow.

Without a word, she walked past me, towards the balcony. I followed with my eyes, watching her silhouette against the curtains as she pulled them aside and stepped into the warm Catalan night. The sky was velvet black, the Mediterranean just visible in the distance, silver under the moonlight.

I stepped out after her.

She stood with her arms on the railing, gazing out across the dark horizon. The sea was still, calm. And so was she, at least on the outside.

Then she spoke. Quietly.

"I like you," she said, her voice trembling just enough to betray the truth of it. "Damn it, Wesley... I like you." In her very seductive and cute Spanish accent.

I stood beside her, uncertain, full of words but with none of them quite ready.

"Why did this happen?" she asked, not turning her head.

I took a breath. "I don't know," I said honestly. "How could I? But I feel the same."

There was a pause, not awkward, just heavy. A space where two lives were weighing themselves against something neither of us had expected, wanted originally but nature had drawn us close for a reason, it was purely nature.

And then, like a slow wave hitting the shore, it hit me, Lelena. Her scent still clung faintly to my other pillow back in the room. Her laughter was still echoing somewhere inside my mind. She had been here. We'd had two weeks of shared memories, breakfasts, swims, whispers under the covers.

Was I being weak? Or was I being honest?

Had something shifted in me during those weeks that I hadn't noticed? Was there something I'd tried to ignore? Or was this, Sofía, standing beside me in the golden light, simply the kind of rare spark that doesn't ask questions before it appears?

All I knew in that moment was that she was extraordinary, really like someone you imagine but you never feel you will ever meet let alone be with. And that I was completely present. No future, no past, just now.

She disappeared inside for a moment, then returned, holding two glasses of water. "We've had enough wine," she said with a half-smile, handing me one.

We stood together again, the silence settling over us like a blanket.

Then she turned.

Without another word, she leaned in and kissed me. A long, slow, deliberate kiss that left no room for misinterpretation. Her hand rested gently against my chest, and my own moved instinctively to her lower back, pulling her close. She held me there, her breath warm on my neck, her body pressed gently into mine.

"Stay with me, Wesley," she whispered. "Tonight. Just stay. You can leave early, sneak back before anyone's up. But stay now — even if just for company. Please."

Her voice broke ever so slightly on the word please, and in that crack, I heard everything, the loneliness, the longing, the truth we were both too afraid to say out loud. That perhaps, just perhaps, the life we'd both been so carefully living had just been waiting for a moment like this to shatter and become something else, if only for a few days.

I looked at her. And I knew, deep down, that whatever decision I made tonight, it wouldn't be one I'd forget, and I would always have…

We stood quietly on the balcony, the warm Catalan breeze swirling gently around us, carrying the distant scent of jasmine and salt. Sofía turned to me, her eyes reflecting more than just moonlight, they held questions, doubts, emotion.

She spoke softly, almost as if afraid the night might overhear. She told me about her engagement, and marriage arranged for later in the year to someone she had known since school, a man she once thought she loved. But now, she confessed, her feelings for him felt like a distant echo compared to the raw intensity of what had already begun to stir between us.

"How could this ever work?" she whispered. "You might be gone in a few months… and I would be here. Alone. Wondering."

She wrapped her arms around me, her voice catching slightly. A single tear rolled down her cheek. And then, she kissed me. Not once, but again and again, kisses filled with confusion, longing, and something dangerously close to love.

Without another word, she turned and slipped into the room, her steps light and deliberate. The bathroom door clicked shut, and moments later, I heard the soft hiss of the shower. Her voice floated out, playful and calm: "Wesley, I've left a towel for you... come in when I'm done."

I stood a moment longer on the balcony, letting the wind cool my thoughts, before going inside. The room glowed gently with lamplight. When she emerged, her hair wrapped in a towel and her skin dewy and warm, she smiled as she passed me the spare towel.

I took my turn in the shower, a brief moment alone to process everything that had happened and was still happening. When I stepped out, freshly towelled and heart thudding, she was once again on the balcony.

She wore a silk nightie, soft and flowing, her hair now loose around her shoulders. The moonlight caught her perfectly, part dream, part mystery, completely beautiful.

For a second, I genuinely wondered if Sergi had spiked my drink back in the bar and I was laid out somewhere with a bunch of surfboards piled on top of me. But no. This was real. Somehow, this was actually happening.

I wrapped a towel around my waist, still warm from the shower, and folded my clothes neatly onto the chair by the dresser, a habit drilled into me from years of living out of suitcases and staying in hotel accommodation.

As I stepped out onto the balcony, the night wrapped itself around me like a familiar blanket. Sofía didn't turn to look, she just smiled gently, knowing I was there, her arms touching softly balcony rail, gazing out to the moonlit Mediterranean.

In the distance, I could hear faint laughter, a group of tipsy tourists making their way back to the hotel, giggling and staggering, flip-flops slapping against the pavement. It reminded me that just below this quiet cocoon, a whole other world was still moving, breathing, laughing.

Further out, down by the promenade, the quiet hum of the street cleaning brigade had begun. It was a strange nightly ritual I'd grown to appreciate, a symbol of order and renewal. Every night, like clockwork, an army of brushes, hoses, and sleepy men would tidy away the mess of the day, so the Costa Brava could wake looking perfect once again.

We stood in silence for a moment, watching the distant shadows move like dancers through the steam and light. Sofía turned to me, her eyes softer now.

"I love that they clean the streets like that," she said. "It's like nothing bad ever happened here."

"It's Spain," I replied with a half-smile. "Even the chaos gets tidied up eventually."

She chuckled under her breath and leaned her head gently on my shoulder. There was no need for words anymore. Not yet. Just the soft hiss of the sea in the distance, the distant hum of the town, and the steady rhythm of two people standing still in the middle of a storm they hadn't planned on starting.

And yet, here we were.

She reached for my hand, her fingers lacing gently with mine, and without a word, guided me back through the balcony doors and into the dimly lit room. The soft breeze trailed behind us, tugging at the curtains as if reluctant to let us leave the night behind.

Inside, the mood was different, intimate, still, suspended in a kind of quiet magic. The light from a small bedside lamp cast a warm golden glow across the room, dancing softly over the sheets. Sofía turned to face me, her eyes searching mine, not for answers, but for reassurance, for the feeling we both already knew was there.

We kissed, slowly, sweetly, as if time itself had slowed for us. No urgency, no rush, just a shared moment that deepened with every passing breath. Her hands moved to my shoulders, tracing the line of my back with the lightest of touches, as if learning the shape of me by heart.

The bed was cool and welcoming as we slipped under the covers, the sheets brushing against sun-kissed skin. We lay facing each other, inches apart, breath mingling, hearts tapping a rhythm that felt older than us both.

There was no need to speak, not here. Everything that mattered was already being said in the way we moved, the way we held each other, the way we took our time. She brushed a strand of hair from my forehead and smiled, a soft, sleepy smile that held wonder and hesitation all at once.

Outside, the Mediterranean whispered on. But in that room, the only sound that mattered was the slow hush of two souls finding each other in the dark.

Sofía nestled close, her head resting lightly against my chest as our legs found each other beneath the covers. I could feel the soft rhythm of her breathing settle into mine, like we had shared this space for years rather than moments. My arm wrapped around her instinctively, protectively, and she gave the smallest sigh, content, safe, warm.

We didn't rush anything. We didn't need to. Everything unfolded with the gentle elegance of a slow dance. Fingers brushed skin. Lips met again, softer now, slower, like we were writing a love letter with touch instead of words. The tension we'd both carried, from the days, from the months, from the stories that had brought us here, seemed to melt away, replaced by something softer. Something real.

Outside, the street quieted. Even the sea seemed to hush, as if giving us our moment. And inside, time held its breath while two people, lost in circumstance, found in each other, explored a connection that neither had expected, yet both had longed for.

At some point, much later, we simply held one another. She rested her hand on my chest, and I traced small circles on her shoulder. We didn't talk about tomorrow. We didn't speak of what came next. In that moment, nothing else existed but the warmth of the sheets, the scent of her perfume still lingering faintly in the air, and the comfort of knowing, even if just for one night, we weren't alone.

She whispered my name once, barely audible, and then drifted off to sleep, her head on my chest.

And I lay there, staring at the ceiling with the glow of the lamp casting long shadows, wondering how something so simple could feel so powerful, and how one summer could change everything. Sofía was just amazing, I was smitten.

The soft golden light of early morning spilled through the edges of the curtains, casting long, delicate shadows across the bed. The hum of the town had not yet begun, just the occasional chirp of an early bird, the distant shush of the sea, and the slow, steady breathing of Sofía beside me.

Her hand was resting lightly on my chest, our legs gently tangled beneath the linen sheets. The air in the room still held a trace of the evening's warmth, a mix of night breeze, faint perfume, and skin against skin. I lay there for a moment, not moving, barely breathing, afraid that any shift might break whatever spell we had found ourselves under.

She stirred slightly, her fingers brushing across my chest before tucking under her chin. I turned my head to look at her, hair mussed from sleep, lips slightly parted, a softness that made my heart catch just a little. For all the complications, the questions, and the unspoken things still to be dealt with, in that moment everything was simple. There was peace.

I kissed her gently on the forehead, a silent promise, and slowly slipped out of bed, careful not to wake her. She murmured something softly in Spanish, half-asleep, then turned to nestle into the pillow I had left behind.

I padded quietly to the bathroom, freshened up, wrapped myself in the hotel robe, and gathered my things. My clothes were neatly folded, just as I'd prepared the night before, because even in chaos, a good rep never forgets his appearance.

By the time I slipped out into the hallway, the sun was stretching it's arms over the horizon. I made my way to my own room just a few floors doors down and along the corridor, showered quickly, changed, and made notes for the morning welcome jobs at hand in Calella. There was still work to be done. There always was.

An hour later, I returned to the breakfast room, freshly shaven, uniform crisp, trying to appear as though I hadn't just woken up in another world entirely.

And there she was.

Sofía sat near the back, in the same seat she'd favoured before, her coffee in hand, hair now neatly pulled back, wearing a simple cream blouse that somehow looked effortlessly elegant yet again. She glanced up as I entered, and her face broke into a soft smile, not flashy, not seductive, but the kind that settled somewhere in your chest and refused to move.

I crossed the room slowly, as if to not rush the moment, and she set down her cup.

"Bon dia, señor Wesley," she said quietly, her voice warm and tinged with something unspoken.

"Bon dia, señorita Sofía," I replied, smiling as I pulled out the chair beside her. "Sleep well?"

She tilted her head slightly. "Better than I have in a very long time."

And just like that, the morning began, not just with coffee and croissants, but with something gently shifting in the space between us. Something fragile. Something real.

Over breakfast, as the soft clinking of cutlery and quiet morning chatter filled the room, I shared my plans for the day with Sofía.

"I've got a welcome meeting in Calella just after ten," I said, pausing to sip my morning tea with it's creamy goats milk, "and then I'll be bouncing between a few of the hotels. A transfer group's coming in early this evening, not a big one, but enough to throw dinner off schedule. I'll probably be back around eight… if all goes smoothly."

She nodded, her eyes never leaving mine, her fingers tracing the rim of her cup.

"Then we'll have lunch together, also?" she asked, her voice soft, hopeful.

"Lunch, definitely," I smiled. "And dinner, if you don't mind staying near the hotel."

"I don't mind at all," she said, a spark in her eyes. "I'll hold onto that all day. It'll give me something to look forward to while I'm stuck crunching numbers with the reception staff."

We both laughed, the mood light and easy. But beneath it was something more, a kind of warmth that seemed to settle in the space between us. She reached across the table, her hand brushing mine, and whispered, "I haven't smiled like this in a long time, I mean it Wesley, I really have not been this happy for a long time."

And for a moment, the business of the day, the chaos of arrivals, the clipboard filled with schedules, it all faded.

This wasn't just a morning after.

It was something beginning.

As I stood to leave, ready to chase the next ticking hour of my day, she held my gaze and said, "Work happy today, Wesley. I know I will."

I nodded; my grin uncontrollable. "See you at lunch, princesa."

Then I turned, stepped out into the golden light of the morning, and mounted the red moped, the engine sputtering to life with its usual growl, feeling just a little more buoyant than usual, like the whole world had quietly shifted on its axis.

The transfer that afternoon was a busy one. I was up near the French border, standing in the hazy heat of late afternoon, clipboard in hand and smile firmly in place, waiting for the convoy of British coaches to roll in. These weren't your average airport arrivals. These were the hardy adventurers, guests who had spent the best part of one and half days travelling from parts of the UK by road, winding their way through France, across the Pyrenees, and finally into Spain.

I always felt a touch of sympathy for them, stiff from the journey, bleary-eyed, some still smelling faintly of service station chips and long-haul air. But I shouldn't have. Because without fail, when those coach doors opened, and they saw one of us waiting, a rep in a smart shirt with a friendly face, there tired expressions turned to excitement. They were here. The sunshine, the sea, the sangria, it was all ahead of them now.

there adventure had properly begun.

After the handshakes and headcounts, the drop-off circuit began: Lloret de Mar first, then Blanes, Malgrat, Santa Susanna, Pineda and finally Calella. Hotel after hotel, bags unloaded, jokes made, directions given. A small chaos repeated weekly. The kind of organised mayhem only a rep could truly appreciate.

By the time the last guest had disembarked, and the coach turned back toward my own stop, the Altura Park, I was absolutely done in. Running on caffeine and adrenaline, my mind flickering between names, room numbers, emergency procedures... and the fact that someone very special was waiting back at the hotel for me.

Sofía.

That thought alone gave me just enough of a second wind to climb off the coach, dash to my room, and dive into a quick shower. The water hit my back like a jolt of clarity, and I stood there for a moment, letting the tiredness melt off me.

Within ten minutes I was dressed again, my smartest shirt, freshly ironed trousers, a splash of cologne, and my wallet stuffed into my pocket. I gave myself one last look in the mirror, raised an eyebrow at my own reflection (as if to say, really? you?) and headed down.

The bar was already humming with the soft murmur of holidaymakers. Glasses clinked, music drifted in from the terrace, and gentle breeze through the lobby windows.

And there she was.

Sofía.

Hair brushed loose from her shoulders, a glass of wine resting in one hand, her eyes scanning the doorway until they found mine. She smiled. I smiled back. The noise of the bar seemed to fade just slightly. My steps quickened.

Tonight, I wasn't just another rep wrapping up a long day.

Tonight, something altogether different, and unexpected was waiting.

She stood as I approached, her smile warming me more than any Catalonian sun could manage. "You look smart," she said, brushing a speck of imaginary dust from my sleeve. "Busy transfer?"

"You could say that" I chuckled, offering her my arm. "I think my brain's still somewhere between Blanes and Santa Susanna."

We wandered out of the hotel together, past the softly lit pool, now quiet except for the occasional laughter of a few lingering guests and the gentle trickle of water from the fountains. The evening was warm, with the faintest salt breeze coming in from the sea. The world had settled into that perfect Mediterranean hush, not silent, but slowed down.

We made our way along the promenade; towards a little tucked-away restaurant I knew just beyond the usual tourist spots. It was a local place, all rough stone walls, flickering candles in wine bottles, and a blackboard menu in Catalan scrawled with chalk. The owner, a stout man with an apron far too small for him, gave me a wink as he saw us arrive. I had eaten here before several times with Elisabeth the German Representative as friends, but I had ideas the stout man was convinced I was now with someone else, which I was but totally different.

Our table was set outside, beneath a climbing vine tangled with fairy lights, and we sat close. Sofía slipped off her jacket and ordered us both a glass of the house rose fruity, dry, exactly what we needed.

"I asked about you, you know," she said between sips. "After the fire. Everyone said you handled it like a professional."

I shrugged. "It's just part of the job."

"No," she said. "It isn't. Not like that. They said you sorted accommodation for seventy-six people in less than an hour. That's not just a job, Wesley. That's care."

I didn't quite know what to say, so I took another sip of wine and looked out at the darkened horizon.

She leaned in a little closer. "You do care, don't you? About people. That's what I see."

I met her gaze. "I try. But it's not always easy, the British tourists can be incredibly hard work at times and sometimes truthfully, I am not sure we should even let some of them out of the country." She laughed…

We fell into a comfortable silence after that, as our food arrived, paella for her, grilled chicken for me, served with crusty bread and olive oil that tasted like it had been pressed that morning.

As we ate, we talked about home, family, what we missed. She told me about her childhood outside Tarragona, her schooling, her fiancé, a man she'd known for years, someone good and stable, but safe. to safe, maybe.

"There's no spark," she said, quietly, "not like this. I don't even know where this is going, but I feel it — with you. And that terrifies me."

I reached out and took her hand. "You're not the only one."

By the time dessert came, a simple flan and two small coffees, the world had folded in around just the two of us. Street noise faded, other diners disappeared into background blur, and the hours passed without effort. When we rose to leave, the owner waved us off like old friends, pressing a bottle of wine into my hand "for the lady."

We walked slowly back to the hotel under a blanket of stars. The Mediterranean stretched beside us, black and endless, the lights of the beach bars reflected in its surface. As we neared the hotel entrance, Sofía stopped.

"Let's sit for a moment," she said, gesturing to a stone bench tucked beneath a palm.

We sat. She looked at me, her expression softer now.

"This can't work, you know," she said quietly. "You'll be gone in a few months. And I'm supposed to be married by Christmas."

I didn't say anything at first. I just held her hand.

She looked away, a tear escaping down her cheek. "But it doesn't stop how I feel."

I reached out and brushed the tear away. "Nor me."

She turned to me then, full of emotion, and kissed me with a kind of urgency that said everything words couldn't. When we stood, she didn't let go of my hand until we were inside the hotel once more.

The hotel lobby was quiet at this hour, the night porter half-dozing behind the desk, and the lights dimmed to a soft glow. Our footsteps echoed softly on the cool, white marble tiles, flecked with grey like scattered whispers of ash, polished so smooth they reflected the chandeliers above like pools of moonlight.

We said nothing as we walked, her hand in mine, the silence between us not awkward at all but charged, alive with something unspoken. As we reached her corridor, the sound of our steps was crisp, the marble giving no place to hide nerves or hesitation.

Outside her room, she turned to me as she had the night before. The key trembled slightly in her hand.

"I should say goodnight," she said, her voice barely more than a breath.

I nodded gently, but I didn't move. Neither did she.

Then came the faintest smile. The kind that says I know I shouldn't... but I want too anyway. She turned the key, and with a soft click, the door opened.

She stepped inside and looked back. "Come in, Wesley," she said, her voice velvet in the low light.

Inside, the air was warm, scented faintly with her perfume and the salt of the Mediterranean drifting through the open balcony doors. The marble tiles continued through the room, cool and clean beneath our feet. She slipped out of her shoes with a grace that felt choreographed, then smiled over her shoulder and disappeared into the bathroom.

"I'll be just a minute," she called.

I exhaled slowly and removed my shirt, folding it with care over the armchair. The hush of water running behind the bathroom door played like background music to my thoughts. I sipped a little water from the glass by the bed, the clink against my teeth sounding unusually loud in the stillness.

When the door finally opened, time paused.

She stood in the doorway, her hair damp and falling in soft waves, her body wrapped in a flowing silk nightgown the same as the night before that shimmered slightly as she moved. The contrast of her skin against the pale fabric was striking, and for a moment, I couldn't find breath, let alone words.

She said nothing, only walked past me toward the balcony. I followed.

Outside, the town had gone quiet. Far below, the gentle hum of street cleaners swept again through the resort like a lullaby for the city. A few drunken tourists wandered by laughter bouncing off the stone façades. But up here, on that private slice of marble paradise, we were in our own world.

Sofía leaned against the rail, arms resting gently, her silhouette caught in the moonlight.

"I don't know how we got here," she whispered, not looking at me. "I'm supposed to be marrying someone. Someone I... care for, yes. But this" she turned now, meeting my eyes, "this feels like the truth. And that frightens me."

I stepped beside her, towel wrapped at my waist, the evening breeze brushing against our skin. "It frightens me to," I said honestly. "But I'm here. And I feel it to, and it's been an amazing surprise."

She reached for my hand, fingers interlacing slowly, then drew close. Her lips found mine once again, not hurried, not uncertain. Just real. She kissed me like someone letting go of every barrier. And I kissed her back the same way.

We moved inside, still hand in hand.

The bed was cool with the weight of night. We slipped beneath the covers as if entering something sacred. Her skin was soft beneath my touch, her breath warm against my neck. Everything slowed. Everything mattered.

That night, we didn't just undress, we unravelled. Every whisper, every touch, every heartbeat was a sentence in a language only the two of us knew. There were no language barriers, no cultural differences and no expectations.

Outside, the moon moved on. But in that room, time folded in on itself, as if the world had paused just for us. I knew I just wanted it to loop in time itself.

The morning came slowly.

Light crept into the room in soft, golden strokes, filtered through gauzy curtains that fluttered in the sea breeze. The marble tiles beneath the bed were cool once more, reflecting the pale pinks and early blues of the waking day. Outside, the first sounds of life were beginning, a delivery truck rumbling down the street, a distant bark of a dog, and the melodic clatter of breakfast plates being set downstairs in the restaurant near the poolside.

I stirred first, my eyes adjusting to the soft light. For a moment, I wasn't quite sure where I was, until I turned and saw her beside me.

Sofía.

Her dark hair spread like ink across the pillow, one arm tucked under her head, her breathing deep and even. The silk nightgown lay like a whisper against her skin. Peaceful. Serene. And mine, if only for this moment.

I lay there, watching her sleep, reluctant to disturb the stillness. But duty, always faithful, tugged at me. I had a morning meeting at a hotel in Santa Susanna for another overseas representative that I was covering, and I needed to be back in my room, dressed, ready, and composed.

Quietly, I slid out from under the sheet, feet finding the chill of the marble below. I dressed in the dim light.

As I gathered my things, she stirred.

Her eyes opened slowly, a sleepy smile tugging at the corner of her lips. "You're going?"

I nodded gently. "Work calls."

She reached for my hand, still half-asleep. "Will you come back later?"

I leaned down, kissed her softly on the forehead. "Lunch, remember? I'll be back, and we'll have the afternoon... before you leave to go back to Tarragona."

She smiled. "I'll hold you to that."

I left the room with my heart full, and a strange mix of exhilaration and apprehension chasing me down the corridor. Behind me, the door clicked shut. Ahead, the day was already beginning.

By the time I passed the reception desk, the hotel was stirring with activity. I nodded at Manuel, the barman, who was in the lobby who gave me a sly wink and simply said, "Buenos días, Casanova."

I rolled my eyes, but couldn't help the grin that followed, maybe I was the real Casanova after all.

Back to being the rep. Back to the heat, the complaints, the coaches, the calls.

But something was different now. I carried her with me, not just the memory of the night, but the feeling that perhaps, for once, I wasn't just living in someone else's story.

This one might be mine.

A Ride Through Familiar Roads

Shooting along on my red moped was always great fun, and I loved the journey out of Pineda towards Santa Susanna as I passed some open ground and farmland on my left and the sea on my right. I also got the chance to quickly check the first surf spot I had surfed in the region, that always gave me a buzz. Remember, once a surfer, always a surfer. I get mesmerised by swell lines and surf; I look for them everywhere, even in lakes at a micro level. It's crazy, really.

The hotel I was covering that morning was a big one, hosting a couple hundred Cosmos guests, so I was pleased. It meant a busy morning, nothing boring and a welcome distraction from dwelling too much on my thoughts from the past week or two. Mentally, I was in a good spot.

Suddenly, a double beep 'beep beep!' came from the opposite side of the road. It was Elisabeth, the German rep, shooting past in her little car. Her arm was out the window, waving wildly, a big grin on her face. 'Guten Morgen, Wesley!' she called out as she zipped by, looking beautiful as ever.

I didn't dare shout back, I was at top moped speed, and worried that if I opened my mouth, I'd end up swallowing a fly, so I just waved enthusiastically. These quick, happy exchanges between reps had become a routine, part of the daily rhythm. Everyone was always dashing off somewhere, but there was always time for a grin and a wave. It was one of the little things that made life in resort feel like a big, bizarre family.

A Midday Detour

After finishing up my morning duties, it was time to shoot back to my home at the hotel for some well-earned downtime. But before heading straight there, I decided to make a little detour to the beach and see the lads at the lifeguard tower. True to form, there they were, the whole lot of them, lounging around like a Mediterranean version of Baywatch, minus the running.

Even Sergi was there, which always made me chuckle. Did he ever stay open for more than a couple of hours at a time? But then I realised his surf shop was more of an evening affair; his customers were mostly working locals or business owners who popped in later in the day. That was how life ticked along here.

Mateo was already barefoot, shirtless, and sipping something cold from a bottle. He'd just finished a morning at his market stall in Pineda. He was a proper character, that one, a market trader with charm oozing out of every pore, and a salesman to rival any Del Boy. His stall was right along the seafront, packed full of gorgeous leather goods, belts, bags, purses, and those dreamy Spanish sandals that seemed to last forever. Some of the stock came from North Africa, some handcrafted in Spain, but all of it beautifully made.

I had a quick chat with the gang, catching up on the gossip, mostly surf talk and harmless beach banter, before promising I might swing by again later. Then I hopped back on the red devil and zipped off along the beach road, weaving between the morning rush of tourists now trickling onto the beach like sleepy ants.

Inflatable sunbeds, neon rubber rings, blow-up crocodiles and beach balls… it was like dodging an obstacle course designed by a seven-year-old. Still, there was something joyous about it all. The excitement in the air, the scent of sea spray mixed with coconut sunscreen, it never got old.

Just a few more minutes, and I'd be back at Altura Park — my sanctuary, my base, my little corner of this chaotic slice of Catalonia.

The Farewell Walk

I met Sofía at the poolside bar, just as the sun began to dip lazily behind a cloud, the only cloud in the sky. She was already seated, poised, elegant, and looking more professional than ever. Immaculately dressed, her dark hair drawn back with subtle sophistication, and yet her smile… her smile was radiant enough to make anyone forget the heat, the chaos, the world beyond that moment.

As I walked up, the waiters behind the bar looked up and gave me a wave, a couple even threw me a cheeky grin and one of those exaggerated hand signals that clearly meant "¡Guapa!" I ignored them, brushing off the banter with a half-smile and a shake of the head. It was par for the course now. They saw something I still hadn't fully processed.

"Hola, Wesley," she said, giving me that soft wave with her fingers and a look that carried a dozen unspoken things. "Good day for you?"

"Yes," I replied, "and for you?"

"It's been lovely," she said, her voice quiet and calm. "But I must go home soon. Catch the train."

I nodded, trying not to betray the tiny knot forming in my stomach. "Let's have a drink then," I said. "Maybe a bite to eat, and I'll walk with you to the station."

"That would be nice, my love," she replied, and for a second, everything felt like the first pages of a novel you don't want to end.

We sat, we ate, we talked, but both of us knew. The signs were there. I could feel it in her eyes, in the soft pauses between our words. This wasn't just goodbye for the week. There was a weight hanging over us, gentle but sure, like the end of a summer storm. I knew it. She knew it. And perhaps, in the most human of ways, neither of us had the courage to say it aloud.

As we set off along the beach path toward the train station, I couldn't help but comment on how beautiful she looked. "Even more than yesterday," I said. "And yesterday, you were already extraordinary."

Her cheeks flushed the sweetest shade of rose. "Stop it," she laughed. "I'm the lucky one, being walked to the train by a charming English gentleman. It's so old-fashioned. I like it."

I offered to take the road, it was quicker, cleaner, far less likely to draw attention. But she insisted on the beach path. Of course she did. It was more romantic, more us. I knew what that meant, it meant walking straight past the lifeguard tower.

Sure enough, like a scene from a comedy sketch, I saw motion at the tower. Mateo was up in his perch, swinging his binoculars straight toward us. Within seconds, the others were nudging each other, a line forming, hands waving. One was already miming a dramatic swoon.

"Friends of yours, Wesley?" she asked, with a smirk.

"Si," I replied. "Very good friends, actually."

"They look very happy to see us."

"Oh, I think they're just amazed someone like you is willingly walking alongside someone like me."

She laughed. "No no — I'm the lucky one, remember?"

The train was already pulling in by the time we reached the platform. I carried her case to the side, and we stood together in silence, the sound of the sea just behind us and the screech of the brakes ahead. I hugged her close, kissed her softly, and saw tears forming in the corners of her eyes.

We didn't say much. We didn't need to.

"I'll call you," I said.

"Si, Wesley. Please. That would be nice."

And then she was gone, into the carriage, into the crowd, into the hum of train doors closing.

I stood there for a long moment before walking back toward the lifeguard tower, feeling oddly like I'd just stepped out of a film, the credit's rolling behind me.

As expected, the lads were waiting. Cheers, hoots, slaps on the back. They circled around like kids at a campfire, waiting for the juicy details.

When I finally told them who she was, Sergi's eyes widened. "You know who she is, don't you, Wesley? Her family is one of the richest in Tarragona. She's practically Catalan royalty. She's in the magazines all the time."

I let out a long breath, smiled faintly and replied, "Well then… for a little while, I guess I was with a princess."

Then I headed home, heart a little heavier, but strangely at peace. As I stepped into the quiet of my room, I could already hear the hotel cleaners shouting their usual chorus from the floors above:

"Hola, Wesley!"

there laughter rang out like bells — familiar, grounding, real.

And just like that, life moved on.

Chapter 10

One of the lesser-known truths about life as a rep overseas is this; time doesn't wait for anyone, not for reflection, not for nostalgia, not even for romance. It barrels forward like a Mediterranean express, no stops, no delays, no apologies. Life doesn't arrive in neatly wrapped chapters; it arrives in waves. One after another.

As the summer deepened, everything moved faster. Faces blurred past me, guests arriving, departing, smiling, complaining, thanking, forgetting. Names dissolved into room numbers; room numbers became departure times. You find yourself waving off people you only just met and wondering whether you ever knew them at all.

Don't get me wrong, I loved my job. I was good at it. But even sunshine and sea air can become exhausting when paired with relentless grinning and the thousand tiny tasks of keeping a holiday on track. Smiling, believe it or not, can hurt. Especially when it becomes your full-time uniform.

And in the midst of this carefully curated chaos, I had my own life to navigate or more accurately, to try and keep afloat. Love had come and gone like a summer storm: intense, beautiful, and fleeting. And just as I began to find my rhythm again, came another force I could never have predicted…

Letters. From home.

You might think this comforting, sweet even, but these weren't the occasional "Hope you're well" scribbles. Oh no. My mother had taken it upon herself to become the official chronicler of Whitstable life. Each letter was a novella of neighbourhood gossip, hedge trimming updates, Cat's antics, and long reflections on what flowers were doing well this year.

And because Spanish post at the time could give snails a run for their money, I didn't receive them daily. They came in batches. Six at once. Eight, sometimes. Like an emotional ambush from another universe. The reception team joked I was being bombed by the British postal service. They weren't wrong.

"Another collection from the UK," joked Rosa, the morning receptionist, handing over a bundle one day. "Your mum writes more than your girlfriend," she added with a wink.

"She's winning on volume, not content," I muttered, smiling.

Of course, Mum meant well. She was trying to connect. But those letters, in all there innocent English charm, became a kind of slow-drip homesickness serum. A reminder of a life that no longer quite fit, of roots trying to pull me back into the soil while I was still flying through the air.

And then... just when I thought the week couldn't get any stranger, it did.

Back at the hotel, the Altura Park, my little home and kingdom, something shifted. A different kind of buzz took hold. Staff were on edge, overly polite, cleaning with double the vigour. The maids started fluffing pillows like their jobs depended on it. The bar staff were polishing glasses that were already spotless. The chef ordered imported olives.

I raised an eyebrow at reception.

"What's going on?"

"We have… a special family arriving," said the receptionist, lowering her voice like a priest revealing a parish scandal. "They take the entire top floor. Every year."

"What sort of family?" I asked.

She gave a vague shrug and a smile that said everything and nothing all at once.

"You'll see."

And just like that, the atmosphere changed. My usual world of smiling tourists, sunburnt families, and moaning about beach towels was about to welcome something else entirely. Something with sharp suit's, darker sunglasses, and perhaps a taste for vintage Chianti...

It was an incredible sight.

They didn't just arrive; they made an entrance.

A fleet of black Mercedes rolled up to the Altura Park entrance like a presidential convoy, sweeping in with that effortless, unmistakable Italian style. The engines barely purred, but the aura was thunderous. Out stepped an entourage that looked straight out of a Fellini film crossed with The Godfather — only this wasn't fiction. This was happening, right here in Pineda de Mar.

I happened to be standing behind the reception desk at that moment, sipping a coffee, going over a transfer list, and wondering whether I'd have time for a swim later. I wasn't on duty technically, but I always liked to be in the know. This was a very lucky coincidence. No other reps were around, they were all out in their respective resorts. Which meant I had front-row seats to something extraordinary.

This wasn't just a wealthy family turning up on holiday. This was a movement.

Black suit's. Immaculate tailoring. Dark sunglasses, indoors and out. Grandparents in flowing outfit's, children in matching designer polos, women with silk scarves and big, silent presence. It was fashion. It was precision. It was a statement.

And in the centre of it all, walking with the kind of deliberate calm that made the air standstill, was the head of the family. You didn't need an introduction. You just knew. Stocky, powerful, with silver hair slicked back and a fat cigar between his fingers, he paused in the doorway and surveyed the lobby like he was stepping onto his own private stage.

Then, the hotel manager, normally a rather calm, borderline lazy but always smart man, suddenly sprinted across the lobby. I'd never seen him move so fast. He practically skidded to a halt before the man, extended both hands in greeting, and bowed his head slightly.

"Benvenuti, Signor."

The cigar-wielding patriarch nodded once, said nothing, and stepped forward. Behind him, the rest of the family flowed through the doors like a tide of black silk and polished leather.

The receptionist had all the keys ready, not just a few, but the entire top floor of the hotel. No waiting in line. No passport-checking. No holiday small talk. This was precision arrival. Within minutes, bellboys and porters were whisking Louis Vuitton cases and expensive leather luggage into the lifts. The lobby, which only moments earlier had been filled with the low hum of tourists in sandals, was now a temple of quiet efficiency.

I just stood there, trying not to stare. Trying not to look to British.

But one of the younger men, mid-30s, slick dark hair, blue sunglasses, a cream blazer despite the heat, turned as he passed me. He looked me up and down, then nodded politely.

"Buonasera," he said with a half-smile.

"Evening," I replied, trying not to fumble the word.

And just like that, they disappeared upstairs, leaving behind only the scent of expensive cologne and the soft click of polished shoes on marble.

The receptionist looked at me, wide-eyed.

"You, see?" she whispered. "Special family."

Special, indeed.

What I didn't know then, and I would come to find out very soon, was that their arrival would turn this ordinary hotel, and this very ordinary rep's summer, into something truly unforgettable in regard to my involvement with the family.

You see, as I've referred to previously, I've always been quietly proud of my ability to blend, to shift between the chapters of society like flipping through a well-thumbed book. From the homeless man on a bench in London to the sharply suited businessmen sipping wine in the city squares, I could usually find a way to fall into rhythm.

My mother used to say I was a bit like Walter Mitty, a dreamer who could slip into roles and moments with a little too much ease. But in reality, it was more than daydreaming. It was an instinct, an odd little superpower I had, to make people feel I belonged. As if I was always meant to be there.

I suppose that's what made me good at the job. You can't just be "on stage" when you're a holiday rep — you have to be everything to everyone. The problem solver. The best mate. The smiling face at 3 AM when the coach breaks down in a petrol station near the border. And I had learned early on that the trick wasn't faking it. It was finding something real in every encounter, even if only for a moment.

It was how I'd won over Sofía, without really trying. How I'd earned the respect of Sergi, Bruno and the others in the local surf scene. And it was why I could eat with German reps at breakfast and chat with old Saga guests in the afternoon without ever feeling out of place.

It was like flicking on a light switch.

That confidence, or chameleon-like calm, whatever you want to call it, would soon become essential, because this Italian family didn't operate in the usual holidaymaker circles. They were something else entirely.

I don't mean they were mafia, I mean, who actually knows that sort of thing? But there was a gravity to them. A power. Something unspoken. Even the waiters stood straighter around them. And the whispers around the hotel grew louder with every passing hour.

They had taken over the entire top floor. No other guests were allowed up there. They had their own food brought in and a separate eating area. One of the hotel chefs had apparently been asked to cook exclusively for them during their stay, and paid cash for the inconvenience.

It wasn't long before I got the call, several days had passed since the arrival.

Reception rang my room just before dinner. "Señor Wesley, the gentleman from the Italian family... the one with the white blazer? He's asking for you."

"For me?"

"Yes. He said the English man. You."

I wasn't sure what they could possibly want with me, but I buttoned my shirt and made my way downstairs. It was time to flick the switch.

I came to reception and was told I was expected at the front bar, the one that overlooked both the pool and the sea beyond. "They're waiting for you on the beach side," the receptionist said with a knowing smile. Not quite sure who they were, I buttoned my shirt properly, straightened up, and strolled through the buzzing bar like I owned it, tourists clinking glasses, waiters weaving through, the warm hum of another golden afternoon.

As I stepped out onto the terrace, I clocked it straight away, multiple tables pushed together to form a long dining stretch, surrounded by a family who oozed effortless elegance. Casual smart, the kind that isn't bought but inherited. They'd somehow managed to dress down without dressing down, linen, loafers, sunglasses, and that unmistakable Mediterranean poise.

At the centre of it all, a silver-haired gentleman raised his hand toward me, beckoning like a conductor cueing a soloist. Two men stood and made space, guiding me into the chair directly opposite him. He smiled, his eyes sharp and studied, and offered his hand. We exchanged first names, which immediately struck me as calculated intimacy.

Right then, I clicked into gear. I became someone else. Not a rep, not a surfer lad from Kent, but the polished Englishman I could channel when required, the sort of my mother used to call "Walter Mitty." I took on the tone of Bond, minus the tuxedo, but with every inch of British charm. And in the back of my mind, I thought this is it, I'm in a Bond film… and he's Scaramanga. The resemblance wasn't far off, either.

"Wesley," he said with a gravelled purr, "I have spoken to the hotel manager. He speaks well of you. He says you are trustworthy, that you understand the locals, and that you are not like the other… younger, wilder reps working in the hotel." His voice was velvet wrapped around steel.

He leaned in slightly. "I would like to ask you a favour. A simple business arrangement, really. My granddaughter — she is young, vibrant. I want her to enjoy her holiday, see the world beyond our table. But she must be protected. Watched over. No trouble from boys, no… unwanted attention. You understand?"

Then he gestured with two fingers, and as if on cue, she appeared.

She stepped into view with the grace of a ballet dancer, tanned skin, high cheekbones, a cascade of dark hair and the quiet confidence of someone very aware of their effect on others. My estimate? Eighteen, maybe twenty. Her eyes met mine for just a second, and I knew then, this was no ordinary summer favour.

I nodded respectfully and replied, "Sir, I'm a busy man, I work long hours, and I can't promise the moon. But I'll do what I can to make sure she's safe, and that she enjoys her time here.

Not for money. Just… because you asked, and because she deserves it."

He paused, then smiled wide. A rare smile. He drew on his cigar, blew the smoke upward like a flourish, and said, "Wesley, I like you. I like you, English. Come. Dine with us tonight. Sit here in the bar with the family when you wish — you are welcome."

He rose, and I followed. Somehow, somewhere between checking transfers and handing out sangria, I'd just shaken hands with a man who felt like royalty and power in equal measure. Whether I'd just become a protector, a pawn, or something else entirely, I couldn't yet tell.

But I knew one thing for certain: the summer had just taken another wild and very unexpected turn.

Dinner that evening felt like I'd slipped through some velvet curtain and landed in a parallel universe. One minute I was a travel rep zipping around on a red moped dodging inflatable flamingos, the next I was seated at a long table with pressed linen, silver cutlery, and a family so smooth they made the cast of The Godfather look like extras from Hi-de-Hi TV Show in the UK.

The granddaughter, Isabella, I learned, was polite, poised, and spoke relatively good English with that lilting Italian rhythm that made everything sound like poetry. She barely said a word at first, just gave me a faint nod and a shy smile, her eyes cast down in a way that seemed half-demure, half-calculating.

The rest of the family chatted freely in Italian, and although I caught the occasional "Inglese" or "Wesley," I mostly focused on eating slowly, sipping wine, and nodding with the occasional "bene, bene" like I was born into it. Truthfully, I had no idea what was being said, but I didn't need to. It was clear I was being vetted, even if the deal had already been made.

At one point, Isabella leaned in and said quietly, "My grandfather says you are responsible. That is good. I do not want another 'stupid boy.'"

I wasn't entirely sure what to make of that, so I just smiled and replied, "Well, I'll try to be a responsible stupid boy."

She laughed, a proper, unexpected laugh, and suddenly the air between us felt a little less formal.

Over the course of dinner, I watched how the family interacted. It was like a play, every person had their role, there place. Respect was given upwards, care extended downwards. And everything orbited around the grandfather. When he spoke, forks stopped. When he laughed, others joined in. He was the gravity.

At the end of the meal, he stood and raised a glass. "To Wesley," he said in English, grinning at me. "May he keep Isabella out of trouble — or in it, but only a little."

Laughter rippled down the table. Isabella blushed.

And just like that, I had been absorbed into the world of this mysterious, powerful family. Not as a servant. Not as a guest. But somewhere in-between. A trusted outsider.

After dinner, Isabella and I walked slowly along the promenade outside the hotel. The sea was a sheet of ink, the air thick with the scent of salt and suncream, and the moon hung lazily over the water like it had nowhere better to be.

"You have a good reputation here," she said.
"I try," I replied.

She smiled and looked out to sea. "I think this will be a good summer."

I wasn't sure if she meant for her... or for everyone.

After three straight days of transfer runs, welcome meetings, complaint handling, coach reschedules, and a bizarre situation involving a German guest, a cactus, and an unflushed toilet, I was wrecked.

Completely, soul-deep, red-eyed wrecked.

So that evening, when I finally rolled back into the Altura Park on my moped — "Red Devil" rattling like it might combust from exhaustion to, all I wanted was a cold shower and a colder Bacardi and coke. But I had a message waiting for me at reception, folded neatly on the counter like a telegram from another era.

It simply read:
"Wesley, I'm looking forward to tonight. See you soon. — Isabella."

A single sentence, tidy, elegant, just like her. It jolted me awake more than a triple espresso could've. I smiled, stuffed the note in my pocket and headed to change. I wondered what Sofía would think of me taking a woman out, younger but we had hardly spoken and on the phone when we did talk it was clear that was now the past and the future was for me back with Lelena for sure.

Earlier that morning, I'd dropped by the lifeguard tower and given my surf brothers a quick heads-up.

"Tonight, I'm bringing someone with me," I'd told them casually, leaning on the rail with my sunglasses still on.

"Someone?" Bruno had said, grinning already.
"Someone," I repeated firmly. "Her name's Isabella. She's with the Italian family at my hotel."

Sergi arched an eyebrow. "She… single?"

I gave them that look.

"No games tonight, lads. Seriously. No flirting, no shoulder flexing, no outrageous serenades. She's under my watch."

Bruno raised both hands like he was surrendering to the Guardia Civil. "Okay, okay. We'll be good. We'll behave."

Mateo chuckled, "We'll treat her like a nun."

"Don't treat her like a nun," I said. "Just don't treat her like fresh meat either."

They both laughed, and I knew I'd have to keep an eye on them anyway. But deep down, they respected boundaries, when it mattered. Surfers were like that you see, we have each other's back, of course I had not shared much about her family, they may not have agreed, so I just kept it on a need-to-know basis, and they did not need to know!

Now, freshly showered and dressed in a crisp white shirt and light trousers, I made my way down to the lobby.

Isabella was waiting, sitting by the fountain that trickled gently just outside the restaurant doors. She wore a flowing olive-green dress and simple leather sandals. Her hair was swept loosely to one side, and when she stood up to greet me, it was like the air around her shifted.

"You look... lovely," I said.

"You to, Wesley," she smiled. "You look... clean."

We both laughed, it broke the tension.

"You ready to meet some real locals?" I asked, offering her my arm.

"Lead the way, Englishman."

And just like that, we walked out into the night, not just a holiday rep and a guest anymore, but something more intriguing, more delicate.

And somewhere up ahead, waiting in the glow of beach bar lights and the scent of grilled sardines, were my friends, and maybe, a new adventure.

The next morning, I was up earlier than usual, not out of duty, but habit. My body clock was hardwired now to beat the sun. I drifted down to breakfast still in a bit of a daze from the night before, that warm fuzzy feeling of having done something... good. I hoped that the Italian family were happy, Isabella had laughed all evening, and I hadn't once had to break up moves from Mateo, Sergi or Bruno. Miracle, really.

I sipped my coffee slowly in the hotel restaurant, nodding at the staff and waving off a couple of guests who spotted me and began gearing up for the day's activities smiling and so British in appearance, already turning into lobsters, bless them. Once I'd worked through a small mountain of toast and Spanish bacon, I did my usual loop, a few friendly check-ins with the British Cosmos guests near the pool, a visit to the front desk to scan the rooming list, and then, as always, a quick detour to the front beach bar for a breath of sea air.

That's where I saw them.

The Italian family had claimed their usual territory, the beachside terrace shaded by striped awnings and framed with blooming pots of geraniums. They were already on their morning espressos and light conversation, all linen shirts and sunglasses. A few of the younger men nodded at me, and then the old man himself, the patriarch, gestured for me to come over.

"Wesley," he said, standing up as I approached. "Buongiorno, ragazzo. Come, come."

He looked refreshed, the morning light catching the silver in his hair. We shook hands firmly, and he leaned in a little.

"She came back very happy," he said simply. "Very happy. You are a gentleman, as I hoped."

"Thank you, sir," I said. "She was great company — it was a pleasure, truly."

He nodded, then reached into the inside pocket of his light jacket and pulled out a thick envelope, one of those hotel ones you find in the desk of each hotel, and in this case, what looked like half the cash reserves of a small town shoved into it.

He pressed it into my hand.

"I can't accept that," I said instinctively, trying to give it back.

"It's not payment, Wesley," he said, smiling kindly but with an edge of firmness. "It's expenses. You paid for everything last night. Drinks, food... even the taxi. This is not money for work. This is money to enjoy. For you. For your friends. You showed my granddaughter respect, laughter, and kindness. You made her feel alive. That deserves celebration."

I paused, looking down at the envelope. It was thick, thicker than I dared guess. I knew just by the weight of it that this was more than I'd earned in the last three months. Probably more than I'd earn before the season ended.

"You sure?" I said quietly.

He just winked. "Dance, eat, drink. That's an order."

With a respectful nod, I thanked him and left, the envelope tucked safely into the inner pocket of my jacket. As I walked back through the bar, I opened it just slightly and caught a glimpse of the contents.

A lot of pesetas. More zeros than I was used to seeing.

I couldn't help but laugh to myself.

Only in Spain. Only in this life.

And that, I thought, was a day officially redefined.

That envelope changed the shape of my day entirely. I had planned on doing my rounds, ticking through rooming lists and taking notes on poolside parasols that needed replacing or other things that I wanted to highlight to the hotel management in each property — all the things a good rep does. But when you're handed a small fortune by someone who might as well have stepped out of a Coppola film and told to enjoy it, well... who was I to say no?

So, I made a quick stop at the hotel reception, left a message with a few guests, checked in with the manager, and then jumped on the red devil, my beloved moped, and buzzed off towards the beach.

Sergi and Bruno were already camped out under the lifeguard tower, tossing a ball between them and trying to look useful while doing absolutely nothing. I pulled up, kicked the stand down, and waved the envelope at them.

"Boys," I grinned, "we're celebrating."

Bruno raised an eyebrow. "You've finally been promoted to 'international playboy', eh?"

"Better," I said. "We're on Scaramanga's tab." A joke I knew they would not understand.

Within the hour, we had assembled the whole beach crew — Sergi, Bruno, Mateo, a couple of surf girls, and even Elisabeth, the German rep, who turned up in a sarong and sunglasses large enough to count as an architectural feature. We commandeered a cluster of tables at the chiringuito down by the beach, the kind with bamboo roofs and menus written in five languages but still somehow charming.

Pitchers of sangria arrived. Bottles of cava. Plates of grilled sardines, patatas bravas, tomato-rubbed bread and local cheeses. At some point, Sergi tried to order oysters "to look like we had class," but we settled for calamari instead.

Music drifted out from a nearby radio, Spanish pop, soft rock, and the occasional burst of Julio Iglesias. The sun was high, the sky cloudless, and the waves rolled in like a soundtrack written just for us. We laughed, we toasted, we argued about who had the worst sunburn (I won, hands down), and we all tried to avoid talking about real life — because real life could wait.

At one point, I wandered to the shoreline, glass in hand, and just stood there, ankle-deep in the sea. I watched as the gang behind me roared with laughter at something Bruno had said and realised… this was it. This was the essence of why we all came out here, and by that, I mean Overseas Reps. Not for the job, not even just for the sunshine — but for moments like this. For a life so rich in memories that it could bankrupt the soul of anyone who never dared to step outside the lines.

That afternoon faded slowly, like a long exhale after holding your breath for years.

And yes, the envelope was lighter by sundown, but still very substantial, and I had become a legend even more with the locals, for my random celebration of life.

But my heart? My god, it was full.

The Final Night with Isabella

It was a quiet evening, unusually so. The summer sun had finally dipped behind the hills, and a soft golden haze lingered in the air like a memory that refused to leave. I had arranged a table at a tucked-away restaurant, a little local place just beyond the usual tourist haunts. Candlelit, quiet, with a sea breeze rolling gently in from the Mediterranean.

Isabella arrived with the kind of grace that only someone truly unaware of their own beauty could have. Her dress was simple, linen, cream-coloured, but she wore it like royalty. A single flower tucked behind one ear, her long dark hair flowing like the tide.

We greeted one another with the casual familiarity that had grown between us, a cheek kiss, a knowing smile. She asked if we were meeting the others, and I shook my head.

"Not tonight," I said. "Just us. Thought we could have one last quiet evening before you all head off. I booked us something special."

She smiled — a real one, full of curiosity and warmth. "I like that," she said.

We talked. About everything. About nothing. About Italy, and the mountains near her family's home in Milan. She told me about growing up with cousins and maids and family dinners that lasted five hours. About the politics of privilege. About how exhausting it was, always being watched, always expected to become someone, even if you weren't sure who that was yet.

At one point, she leaned forward across the candlelight and said, "Wesley... if I were older, do you think you would have looked at me differently?"

The question hung in the air, suspended like the last note of a love song.

I paused. Not because I didn't know the answer, but because I did.

"I think... in another life, Isabella, maybe. But in this one, I promised your grandfather. And more importantly, I have a girlfriend. You deserve someone who doesn't have to choose."

She sat back, nodding. A flicker of sadness danced behind her smile. "You're a good man, Wesley. too good sometimes."

We toasted, gently, to what was, not to what could have been. There was laughter, too. She teased me about my sunburn. I teased her about the little pout she did when reading menus. And when the bill came, I wouldn't let her grandfather's envelope pay for it.

"This one's from me," I said. "For the memory."

After dinner, we walked slowly along the quiet streets. No grand goodbye. No dramatics. Just two people enjoying the fading light of something sweet, something respectful, something true.

At the door of the hotel, she turned to me. "Thank you, Wesley. For being exactly who you are."

"Always," I replied, offering my hand.

She took it, squeezed gently... and then disappeared inside.

That was the last night we spent together. And that was enough. I had completed my unofficial job, and I sighed gently, kind of sad but also happy, I certainly was never expecting any of this when I came to Costa Brava.

Family Departure

The morning of their departure had a calmness about it, that peculiar hush that hangs in the air before goodbyes. The hotel staff were bustling about with luggage, the occasional wave or nod exchanged with members of the family, but there was no chaos. Just a kind of quiet order, like a well-rehearsed performance being packed away.

I was sitting at the front terrace of the hotel, nursing a cortado and watching the Mediterranean glitter under the morning sun, when I heard the familiar walk on the tiled floor.

It was him, the old man, Isabella's grandfather. Still dressed impeccably, dark sunglasses on, his silver hair combed immaculately. He walked with the kind of authority that didn't need to announce itself.

"Wesley," he said, easing himself into the chair opposite mine with a nod of gratitude. "Expresso?"

I gestured to the waiter and ordered. He nodded approvingly.

"Thank you for everything," he said, in that rich, deliberate tone of his. "My granddaughter… she is happy. You made her happy. You respected her. You honoured my word."

I smiled, unsure how to respond at first. "She's an incredible young woman. It was my pleasure."

He reached into the inside pocket of his blazer and pulled out a small white card — thick, embossed, with nothing but his name, a Milan address, and a phone number in neat gold script.

He slid it across the table to me with a finger. "If you are ever in Milan, you call me. You stay with us — with the family. No hotel. That would be an insult."

I laughed lightly, but he wasn't joking. His expression remained firm, sincere. Then the corner of his mouth twitched into something softer, a smile, perhaps, or just a glint of memory.

"And who knows?" he said, taking a sip of his espresso. "Perhaps Isabella will be older… and maybe the dinners will be a little more… interesting."

I raised an eyebrow, amused and touched all at once. "I'll hold you to that."

"You do that," he said. "And Wesley — one last thing…"

"Yes?"

He reached over and patted my hand, his own rough and cool from the morning breeze. "You're a good man. That's rarer than money. Don't forget it."

And with that, he stood, straightened his jacket, and walked back toward his waiting family where Isabella stood watching. I watched as the fleet of dark cars rolled away once more, the hotel returning slowly to its usual rhythm.

But I sat there a moment longer, the business card still warm from his hand resting in mine and thought: You never know where life will take you. And who it will take with you.

Chapter 11

There are moments when living and working abroad that you start to lose a sense of yourself. Not deliberately, and not all at once, but little by little, chipped away by the sheer intensity of it all. You're constantly on the move, juggling a thousand things at once, and the mental load begins to pile up in ways you don't always notice, until suddenly, you do.

By this stage in the season, every overseas rep begins to feel the strain. I was no different. Flat out, seven days a week, covering not just one resort, but two towns, seven hotel and apartment units, and supporting yet more across neighbouring areas. It's not a sprint, it's a relentless marathon, with no pause button. And back then, in the '80s and '90s, there was no such thing as mental health support. You just got on with it. You kept smiling, you stayed professional, even if inside, you were fraying at the edges.

What people don't always understand is that this job isn't just about happy tourists and suntans. Yes, there are laughs and cocktails and picture-postcard sunsets. But there's also the other side, the difficult guests, the persistent complainers (often, for some mysterious reason, heavily concentrated from the Southeast of England), the dramas, the emergencies.

We dealt with accidents, hotel fires, medical incidents, and yes, deaths. The so-called "shoulder season" in spring and late summer often brought older holidaymakers, and the heat could be unforgiving. That year alone, I handled several deaths, elderly guests who came for a gentle week in the sun and never made it home. There was even an old saying among reps back then: "If there are a few empty seats on the return flight, they're still flying home — just from underneath." Morbid, yes, but it was part of the job.

And it wasn't always the elderly. Peak season brought the young and the reckless. A tragic few who drank too much, choked in their sleep. Or worse, those who made a terrible split-second decision, climbing onto a sixth-floor balcony ledge, daring their mates to watch them leap into the pool below. Misjudging the distance. A scream, a siren, and a dreaded call to my room from hotel security. These weren't isolated incidents. They were the harsh reality of what we sometimes dealt with behind the scenes.

I've a heap of stories I could continue to share with you, tales that stretch the length of the season and beyond. But I'll keep most of them tucked away for now, save for this one, which has never quite left me.

It was late June, and one of my guests had arrived for a ten-day holiday. A lovely chap, elderly, gentle, and content with the simple things. His only plan was to sit by the pool, soak up the atmosphere, and listen to the joyful noise of life buzzing around him. Each morning, without fail, he'd stroll down to the local shop and pick up The Sun, always a day late, of course, as was standard in resort life back then. The bar staff got to know him well. He'd order his usual drink, find his favourite lounger, pop up the umbrella, and let the day unfold.

This particular day was like any other. The pool was alive with the usual chaos, inflatables flying, kids cannonballing, parents pretending to be asleep while secretly watching everything. A classic early-summer day on the Costa Brava.

As the afternoon wore on, families began packing up, heading back to their rooms to shower and prepare for dinner. The bar staff started their evening clean-up. But the old gent was still there, hat tipped forward, stretched out under his umbrella. A peaceful scene.

It wasn't until just after 6 p.m. that one of the waiters gently approached him. "Señor, the bar and pool is closing now." No reply. They lifted the hat from his face, and found he'd passed away, quietly, sometime that morning.

He'd been there all day, sun creeping across his body, slowly baking him in the Mediterranean heat. The kids had splashed and screamed, couples had flirted, sangria had flowed, and all the while, this gentle soul had slipped away, unnoticed, in the heart of the noise.

Now, some might find that tragic. And yes, there's a sadness to it. But there's something beautiful too, in the way he went, sun on his skin, laughter in the air, drink beside him, no fuss, no fear. Just… peace.

I've often said it was as if he simply checked out of life the way he checked into the hotel, politely, quietly, without causing a ripple. And I'll admit, a part of me still chuckles at the irony. He literally cooked by the pool while life carried on around him. Morbid? Maybe. But if you've ever worked a summer season, you'll understand, these things happen, and we all find our way of coping.

You can call it sad, or you can call it poetic, I suppose it depends whether you're a half-pint-full or a half-pint-empty sort of person.

So as the summer waned and the end of the season loomed, I found myself not just physically tired but emotionally worn down. I knew something was shifting inside me. Something that I couldn't quite name yet. But the farewell tour had begun… and I wasn't aware that was the case or even sure I was ready.

Goodbyes That Never Felt Right

Late August had a way of pressing pause on everything. The light was still golden, the sea still warm, the tourists still tanning, but there was something unspoken in the air, the closing act, creeping in at the edges.

I hadn't told many people. Just a few, the ones I couldn't leave without seeing one last time.

I started my goodbyes in the most understated way possible, a quiet nod to the bar staff, a longer-than-usual handshake with Manuel, the barman, who raised his eyebrow with that signature Bond-like moustache twitch and muttered, "You'll be back, Wesley. Spain doesn't let go so easily." I smiled, but inside, I wasn't so sure.

The hotel staff, my extended summer family, took it harder than I expected. The cleaners upstairs called out there usual "Hola Wesley!" but when I told them it was almost over, the smiles dropped. One of them threw a towel at me and said, half-joking, "No te vayas, inglés loco!" — Don't go, crazy Englishman.

Reception was even worse. Lucía — the sweet Catalan receptionist engaged to her St. Albans man, refused to speak to me for a whole morning. When she finally did, she handed over a postcard with a photo of the hotel on it and a message written on the back in perfect English:

"You always made this place more than a hotel. Gracias por todo."

I carried that in my wallet for years.

Sergi and the surf crew took the news in their stride, but I saw the cracks. We didn't do long talks or emotional send-offs. That wasn't the surfer way. Instead, we surfed. My last session on the water was with Sergi, and Bruno. The swell was small, nothing special, but it was ours. We paddled out into the glassy blue, laughing, splashing, catching wave after wave like kids who never wanted to grow up.

When we came in, Sergi walked beside me in silence, then clapped me on the back and said:

"You were one of us. You'll always be one of us."
And that was it.

At the lifeguard tower, the usual banter had been replaced by a strange stillness. Even the binoculars weren't scanning the beach that day. Instead, Mateo called me up the ladder for the first and only time. We sat there, watching the Mediterranean shimmer like a silver sheet, not speaking. Eventually he just said:

"You're leaving a gap, Wes. Just don't forget to fill it with something good."

I said nothing. I couldn't.

And then there were the guests. A few long-stayers, families who had returned year after year and had come to see me not as a rep, but a part of their holiday story. Some left small gifts knowing I was leaving. One couple gave me a framed photo of the view from there balcony, signed on the back: "For the best rep we've ever known." Another just hugged me and whispered, "You mattered."

There was no official send-off, no party, no big farewell tour as the chapter name might suggest. Just dozens of small goodbyes stitched into the fabric of each day. A barista who gave me a free cortado. A performer in Calella who played my song. A lifeguard who handed me a stone from the beach "so you don't forget what the sand feels like."

And somehow... each one broke me just a little bit more.

I didn't cry. Not then. But every goodbye felt like a thread snapping in my chest.

And yet, I still tried to act like I was fine, that this was just another week, another change, another season coming to a close.

But deep down I knew...

This wasn't just the end of a job.
It was the end of a chapter of me.

The Departure

It was just before 10:00 AM when the Cosmos coach pulled up outside the Altura Park Hotel. The Catalan sun was already warming the white and grey marble floors of the lobby, streaks of light bouncing through the glass like the last salute of summer. The staff were in full swing, receptionists typing away, the bar already serving coffee and teas, the maids wheeling past with carts and cheery "hola, Wesley" greetings.

But for me, everything felt muted. Slowed down. Like the volume had been turned low.

My suitcases stood by the front doors, upright and ready, but unwilling, much like myself.

There was no dramatic farewell, no fanfare. Just a few heartfelt hugs from staff, a nod from the night porter who had waited on to see me off, and the gentle hum of the coach's engine outside, idling with quiet urgency. I took a last look at the lobby, the scene of so many mornings, reunions, welcomes, and farewells. It had been my home, my office, my anchor.

The lift door pinged open and out came Manuel from the bar, carrying two small café con leches and a napkin-wrapped bocadillo.

"One for the road, amigo," he said with a wink.

He didn't say goodbye. He just nodded, patted me on the back, and disappeared as quickly as he'd arrived.

Outside, the coach loomed larger than ever. Guests were already boarding, many of them people I'd welcomed to Spain just a week ago. Some smiled warmly as they recognised me. A few waved and whispered as I climbed aboard, "that's our rep!". I wasn't in uniform anymore. Just a well-tanned young man with too many memories stitched into his soul and not enough space in his suitcase.

The driver gave me a respectful nod.

"Final run, eh?" he said, knowingly.
I simply nodded back. "Yep, final run!"

I took a seat by the window halfway down the coach and stared out as the street began to blur into motion. We pulled away from Pineda de Mar slowly, almost hesitantly, as if the place itself didn't want to let go.

The coach wound through the towns I'd come to know so well: Malgrat, Santa Susanna, Calella. Each turn, each beachside bend brought a flicker of memory. The bars, the lifeguard tower, the stretch of sand where I'd walked with Sofía. Each sight was a little dagger, not painful exactly, but sharp with nostalgia.

I saw familiar faces walking the seafront promenade, locals setting up umbrellas, tourists already baking by the beach, oblivious to the silent goodbye playing out behind the coach window.

A couple of guests leaned over from across the aisle,

"You're coming all the way back with us? That's brilliant."

I smiled politely, but inside, my heart ached. Not because I didn't want to be friendly, but because I knew this was it. The real end. The chapter was closing not with drama, but with the quiet creak of a coach door and the hum of tyres against tarmac.

As we moved further up the coast and northward towards France, I could see the line where the summer stopped, the invisible curtain separating the life I'd lived and the one waiting for me beyond.

I was going home. But what I was leaving behind… wasn't just a job. It was me. A version of myself I may never fully find again, and I still had not realised it.

And yet, as Spain receded behind me, the warmth lingered. On my skin, in my bones, and — most of all — in my heart.

Homecoming at Dover

It was early morning when the coach rolled off the ferry and onto British soil, the pale English light casting a soft blue-grey hue over the port at Dover. I'd dozed off during the crossing, lulled by the dull hum of the ferry and the gentle rocking of the Channel. But now I was awake, not refreshed, but… alert. Alert to the fact that this was it.

The long return journey from Spain had reached its final stop.

The coach hissed to a halt and the doors creaked open. Passengers stirred, gathering their bags and stretching their limbs. There was a quiet buzz of reunion in the air, families spotting loved ones, friends waving from car parks, and the unmistakable shiver of the English breeze creeping through the cracks in the coach.

I stood up slowly, reluctant to join the shuffle toward the exit.

As I stepped down onto the tarmac, the first thing I saw was my father's car, pulled in just off to the side. And then there they were, my mum and dad, standing by the boot, both waving enthusiastically.

I made my way over, dragging my bag behind me, trying to appear normal, steady, casual, but inside, I was swimming in a soup of emotions: sadness, pride, regret, nostalgia, and a strange kind of peace that only comes when something momentous finally finishes.

My dad reached me first and gave me a solid hug, clapping me on the back like I'd returned from war.

But it was my mum's reaction that caught me off guard.

She stepped back, looked me up and down, then smiled with that knowing mother's smile, the one that sees past your words and straight into your heart.

"You look like my father," she said softly.

I blinked.

"What?"

She smiled again; eyes misty.

"Your grandfather. The hair — all wavy and strawberry blonde. And that tan. Not a holiday red — a proper healthy golden colour. Just like him when he returned from Africa in World War Two. He was a handsome man, Wesley. You've come home looking like you've lived."

That hit me harder than anything. Because I had lived a lot over the years working in travel. Fully. Madly. Deeply. And now, it showed.

We put the bags in the car. My dad asked about the surfboard, and I told him I'd sold it in Spain. He didn't say much, just nodded and closed the boot. But I knew what he was thinking: something in me had been left behind with it.

The drive home was quiet at first. I stared out at the Kent countryside rolling past the window, green and familiar but somehow not as comforting as it once had been. It felt smaller now, cold, miserable and depressing. As though I had outgrown it just a little during those months on the Costa Brava, for good this time, I mean I had returned lots of time, but it felt different.

But I was home.

Or at least, I was somewhere close. Whitstable, was ahead, and as we descended the large hill, the sea was grey, dismal, and I thought what the hell have I done!

Chapter 12

It didn't take long for the unease to settle in. Within days, hours, if I'm honest, I knew I couldn't stay. Not like this. Not in the quiet stillness of my childhood bedroom in Whitstable, where the wallpaper hadn't changed since the '70s and the silence pressed against the walls like a memory trying to smother you.

The Kentish drizzle outside my window, the Sunday roast routines, the mates in the pub who'd never left the area and couldn't quite comprehend where I'd just been, it all felt like I'd walked back into someone else's life. A life that was still paused in black and white, while mine had just been playing out in full colour under the Catalan sun.

I needed to move. To get out. To chase down something I'd left unfinished. And, of course, my thoughts kept spiralling back to Sofía and the whirlwind of emotion, excitement, and confusion she brought. But that was Spain. And this, well, this was something else entirely.

So, I made the decision. I would go to the Czech Republic. To see Lelena. To try, in some possibly misguided way, to understand whether what we had was ever truly real, or if I had simply been a summer character in the novel of her life. Had she loved me? Or was I just her charming English souvenir?

She was younger, more composed, wrapped in a kind of grace that both mesmerised and unnerved me. I often wondered if I was her boyfriend or her showpiece — someone to parade, but never fully let in. We'd never argued, which once felt like a badge of honour. But now I questioned it — was it peace, or just polite detachment?

So, I packed a bag, booked a ticket, and boarded a coach from Dover bound for Praha. It wasn't glamorous, a 20-something-hour ride, knees crushed, with the scent of stale crisps and yesterday's perfume in the air. But I welcomed the discomfort. In some strange way, it felt right — a journey into the unknown that might answer something unresolved in my soul.

From Prague, I would take the train south to České Budějovice, where her brother had generously offered me a place to stay. He mentioned I could take the local bus to Český Krumlov to see her regularly. I thanked him. But deep down, something didn't sit right. I had always stayed with her before — shared her space, her time, her life. So why now this gentle push into the periphery?

Of course, looking back, I see it now for what it was. Spain had exhausted me, emotionally, physically, and I had arrived in the Czech Republic thinking I was still invincible. I was unemployed, heart-worn, running on adrenaline and a sense of purpose I hadn't quite defined. I had convinced myself this was the answer that maybe I could rekindle something, maybe even start a life here.

But the obvious was waiting just around the bend, the slow unravelling of a love that, in truth, had ended the moment I stepped off that coach in Dover from Spain. And what followed was messy. Painful. A break-up I didn't see coming… and wasn't prepared for in the slightest.

You see, it wasn't just the heartbreak of losing someone I'd loved, truly loved, for the first time in my life. It was more than that. It was the weight of everything I'd sacrificed to be there. Spain. My friends. The job I was brilliant at. The life I had carved out for myself under the sun, all abandoned for the chance to see if what we had was something worth chasing.

And yet, none of it seemed to matter.

My gesture, my leap of faith, was met not with gratitude, not even with grace, but with indifference. As if I were an old beach towel, flung aside once it had served its purpose.

That's what stung the most. Not the rejection, but the realisation that I'd gambled everything... and played the fool.

My world had cracked and shifted, all because of a decision I'd made with the best of intentions but too rash and harshly. Leaving Spain early had been an error, and it had cost me more than I ever imagined. I knew I had been replaced at the resort by some new overseas rep pleased to have a chance.

And so, the plan was made for me to return home.

I came to understand something unexpected about myself during that time, I was a sponge. A quiet absorber of everything around me. The noise, the colour, the chaos of travel, the laughter, the loss. Over the years, I'd taken in so much, sights, emotions, people, that somewhere along the line, I'd stopped wringing myself out. I'd grown numb to certain things, even to death at times, and that realisation unsettled me deeply. Because if you lose the ability to feel, to really feel, then aren't you at risk of losing yourself entirely?

So, there I was again, on the road back to England, for the second time in just a matter of weeks. From the outside, it must have looked like I'd detonated my own life, walked away from a dream job, burned through a love story, and now headed home with my tail between my legs.

But here's the thing: I wasn't broken. I was simply… exhausted. Mentally. Emotionally. Spiritually.

In today's world, I think someone would have seen that. A company might have offered a pause, a couple of weeks to breathe, to rest, to reset. But this was the 1990s, and back then, the machine didn't stop for anyone. I'd gone full throttle in the travel industry from leaving school, never letting up, and this season was no different. Yes, I had lived, fully, but it was constant motion, and constant motion wears the soul thin.

And there was something else: I hadn't been surfing much.

In the heat of summer, the Mediterranean turns fickle. The swells dry up. And for someone like me, that board isn't just fibreglass and wax, it's medicine for the soul and mind. My release. My connection to something that asks nothing of me, except presence. Without it, I'd been bottling everything inside.

And bottles, eventually, break.

Knowing I wasn't broken was a milestone I didn't see coming. It was quiet, not triumphant, but vital. Because realising I wasn't broken meant I could be repaired. Not rebuilt, not started over, just… sorted out. I had some sorting to do, and at least now I knew it.

There's a moment, just before the wheels touch tarmac, or the ferry kisses the dock, or in my case, as the coach rolls off the ramp onto British soil, when it hits you: you're home. And yet, somehow, you're not. To be perfectly honest, I don't think I've truly come home since.

That's exactly how it felt stepping off the coach in Dover.

It was a crisp, grey morning, the kind where your breath fogs the air, and the cold lingers in your bones. The sky above the Channel wore its dullest coat, stitched thick with clouds like they'd been hung there just for me. After months under Mediterranean light, England's muted tones felt like a curtain closing. Comforting, perhaps — but also suffocating.

My parents were waiting at the terminal.

My mum, ever the optimist, was beaming, for her, a drive to Dover was just shy of international travel. She waved with both hands, cheeks pink from the chill, a smile that tried to say everything was fine. My dad stood a little behind, arms folded, his expression soft but unreadable, always present.

And there I was: back in Kent. No job. No plan. Just a suitcase of creased clothes and a head full of second thoughts.

The streets I'd once known by heart felt like strangers now. Familiar shopfronts of Whitstable had become theatrical backdrops to a version of life I no longer recognised. Everything moved slower. Quieter. Like someone had turned down the volume on the world and no one had noticed but me.

But life doesn't wait for anyone.

Within a week, I'd slid back into something resembling a routine, helping around the house, popping into the pub, saying the right things to the right people. Friday and Saturday night pints. Sunday lunch down the pub. Conversations about rent and MOTs and stories from the office. I nodded. Smiled. Laughed in the right places. But I wasn't really there.

I was still in Spain, barefoot on a beach. Still smelling the night jasmine. Still watching the sunrise over Costa Brava rooftops. Still wondering if all of it had actually happened.

The strangest part? I had everything back, my town, my friends, my bed. But none of it fit anymore. I had outgrown the skin I'd once called home. In fact, I did not realise then, but this would be the last real time I ever lived at home again with my parents.

On paper, I was doing what I should, rejoining the familiar. But in my heart, I was elsewhere. A dreamer with sand still in his shoes.

You see, I was always meant to live abroad. I wasn't built for drizzle and hedgerows. I was built for sunlight, heat, and the kind of life where the unexpected could walk through the door at any moment, in the form of a person, or a plan, or a great story waiting to be lived. I knew that if I stayed in England, I would be half the man I was and I certainly did not want to become boring.

Even growing up, there were signs. Living on the Kent coast gave me a few unique privileges. For one, we could tune into French radio on the medium and longwave. I remember laying in the bath or on my bed as a teenager, letting the foreign voices drift in — not understanding much, but feeling somehow more worldly just by listening. It made my hometown feel… connected.

And then there was the youth club, the social melting pot of seaside adolescence. We were sixty-plus miles from London, but a magnet for foreign exchange students. One week it would be the French. The next, Spanish, the Italians or Germans. They came to stay with local families, and inevitably, they ended up at the youth centre. We'd play football — England vs. France one week, the World Cup final the next against Germany. Then in the evenings, we'd flirt and fumble through cross-cultural courtships along the beach front. European girls seemed older, bolder. They were mature beyond their years — or maybe it just felt that way because their worlds were larger than ours.

Looking back now, I realise I was always reaching outward. Always drawn to people from other countries, to languages I didn't yet speak, to stories I hadn't yet lived.

That wanderlust wasn't something I learned abroad, it was always in me. Working overseas in travel simply brought it to life.

I remember one quiet morning, sorting through the few things I'd brought back, I found a pebble from the beach in Pineda. I had tucked it into my bag one day, absentmindedly. Holding it now, thousands of miles away, it felt heavier than it should have, like it carried the weight of an entire season.

Then, one afternoon, the phone rang.

It was the head office at Cosmos. I had called them a week earlier, checking in, staying visible, letting them know I am here. They liked me, I knew that they often laughed with my happy attitude on the phone, plus I had a good reputation of being professional and I knew these qualities are hard to find. I could hear the regret in their voice when they told me there were no placements left for the remainder of the summer or the new winter season. "Stay in touch," they said. "Next spring, we'll find something probably back in Costa Brava for you, if you would like."

But this time, it was different.

"Dominican Republic," she said.

My breath caught.

"Winter season. We're building a new team from scratch. We think you'd be a great fit. You'd be running the show."

I blinked. "When?"

"Next week. You'll need to get your jabs, sort your papers. It's fast, Wesley — but it's real, it's a great opportunity."

The spark reignited, sharp and sudden. The promise of sun, sea, new stories. Something about it felt right... but the weight of the year still sat heavy on my shoulders.

I told them I needed to think. I'd call back.

Later, I walked the beach of Whitstable. The wind was fierce, tugging at my coat like it wanted answers to. The sea was restless, waves crashing against the pebbles like they were trying to speak for me.

I thought about Spain.
About Sofía.
About that pink Seat Panda, the surf, the markets, the morning chats with Elisabeth, the fire, the guests I'd cared for like family and even those I had lost too.
About who I was — and who I was becoming.

I sat on a weather-worn bench overlooking the water. The same beach I used to sit on as a schoolboy, then as a teenager — dreaming of faraway places and big adventures. Funny how life comes full circle. But this time, I wasn't dreaming. I was remembering.

I may have left Spain to soon. In fact, I knew I had.
I may have chased the wrong girl. That was very clear.
I may have lost a version of myself I deeply loved.

But maybe, just maybe… I was exactly where I needed to be, or was I?

Because the story wasn't over yet… an opportunity had been thrown my way.

I stood up from the beach, the wind now softening, the sea calming just a little, as if it too was pausing for a decision. The pebble from Pineda sat in my pocket, warm from my hand. I turned it over in my fingers, weighing its smooth surface against the weight of everything it meant. Another season? Another country? Or was it time to finally settle back in the UK, to breathe, to let the sun set on this chapter for good? I didn't know. Not yet. I made my way home where I knew the phone sat in the hallway where it had always been, waiting.

So was the future. Another season? Another country?...

Acknowledgements

I would like to dedicate this book in memory of my late father, who passed away on 24 January 2024. His unwavering belief in me remains a guiding light. To my dear mother, still with us and still reminding me who I am — thank you for your endless love and encouragement.

To my wife, who has loved and stood by me through the many storms, particularly during recent health scares — your strength, and quiet support made this book possible. To my daughter, Arabella, and my son, Thomas — your love, laughter, and belief in me mean more than I could ever express.

To all my friends in Spain and across my career — especially those in Pineda de Mar, Santa Susanna, Calella and beyond — you brought colour and chaos to every day and gave me memories that shaped a life. To my Italian acquaintances, whose presence added depth and fascination to my time there — thank you.

To the most incredible administration staff, managers, receptionists, bar staff, waiters and of course the maids at every hotel or apartment I worked in my career overseas, your kindness, humour and hospitality will never be forgotten.

To my German representative friend — wherever life has taken you, thank you for the laughter and gentle wisdom during long breakfasts and longer days. We had some great times.

To my special Señorita — wherever you are now, thank you — with warmth, respect, and a silent toast to what once was, and I hope you continue to smile. It was magical and perfection.

…

To Chris Conway of Conway and Sons in Whitstable — thank you for so generously hosting the Echoes of a Season book launch. I'm deeply grateful. You've been one of my oldest and truest friends, and here's to the memories we've made — plus the ones still to come.

And finally, to you the reader — for joining me in these echoes of a season. This story is as much yours as it is mine, I hope you truly enjoyed it, thank you for taking the time to read it and to feel part of it – I hope you laughed some too.

Where the Journey Continues...

As the sun sets on these pages, it rises again over the golden coastline of Catalonia — a land of passion, poetry, and unforgettable seasons. From the soft sands of Pineda de Mar to the spirited plazas of Girona and the timeless charm of Barcelona, the region pulses with life, history, and warmth.

If this book stirred something in you — a longing for Mediterranean light, the taste of sangria at sunset, the laughter of strangers becoming friends — then perhaps it's time to create your own story beneath the Catalan sun.

Explore Catalonia

Discover more about this stunning region through the official travel guide: www.catalunya.com

Travel Inspiration

For travel articles, guides, and ideas to spark your next adventure, visit: www.purevacations.com

Book Your Experience

Specialist travel packages and unforgettable journeys across Catalonia and beyond, curated by those who've lived it. www.pureonetravel.com

Because some stories are just waiting to be lived...

"Els records són l'equipatge que sempre portem al cor."

(Memories are the luggage we always carry in our hearts).

Printed in Great Britain
by Amazon